HEALING THE PARENT CHILD BOND

Healing the Parent Child Bond

HARPER GREENE

Contents

Dedication

Healing the Parent-Child Bond: A Guide to Open Communication and Breaking Generational Trauma

This book is dedicated to the countless parents who bravely confront their pasts to build brighter futures for their children. Your courage inspires us all. It is also dedicated to the children, the resilient inheritors of our legacies, who deserve the gift of a nurturing and supportive family environment.

May these pages offer a beacon of hope and a roadmap towards healing and stronger connections, breaking the chains of intergenerational trauma and forging pathways to a more loving and supportive family life.

This work is a testament to the enduring power of human resilience, the transformative capacity of self-awareness, and the unwavering strength found in familial bonds when nurtured with compassion and understanding. To those who seek solace, understanding, and practical tools to mend fractured relationships and cultivate healthier family dynamics, this book is for you.

May it be a source of comfort, empowerment, and a guiding light on your journey towards healing. Know that you are not alone, and that healing is possible.

Preface

Too often, parents unknowingly perpetuate unhealthy patterns, transmitting the weight of their own trauma to their children. This book is born from a deep understanding of this cycle and a fervent belief in the power of healing and transformation.

Within these pages, you will find not just theoretical knowledge, but practical tools and strategies to break free from these damaging patterns. We delve into the science behind intergenerational trauma, exploring how unresolved pain and trauma are passed down through families, affecting communication, emotional regulation, and overall well- being.

Yet, the book also emphasizes the immense capacity for healing and the possibility of creating healthier family dynamics. Through relatable stories, research-based insights, and actionable exercises, we illuminate the path towards a more harmonious and nurturing family environment.

This is more than just a self-help guide; it's an invitation to embark on a journey of self-discovery, fostering empathy, and building stronger parent-child relationships. The goal is not only to heal the wounds of the past but to create a legacy of well-being for future generations, empowering parents to become agents of change within their own families. We hope this book will serve as a reliable companion, providing support and guidance as you navigate the complexities of intergenerational trauma and cultivate a more loving and resilient family life.

Introduction

This book offers a compassionate and practical guide for parents seeking to heal their relationship with their children and ultimately break free from the insidious cycle of generational trauma.

We acknowledge the profound influence of past experiences on present-day parenting and provide a roadmap towards healthier communication, stronger bonds, and more positive family dynamics. Understanding the legacy of trauma is paramount. Many parents unknowingly repeat patterns from their own childhoods, passing down unresolved pain and impacting their ability to connect meaningfully with their children.

This can manifest in various ways, from difficulty expressing emotions to struggles with conflict resolution and setting healthy boundaries. This book explores the mechanisms of intergenerational trauma transmission, explaining how unresolved experiences can shape our parenting styles, impacting everything from our communication patterns to our emotional regulation.

However, the message of this book is one of hope and empowerment. It's crucial to remember that healing is possible, and that by understanding the roots of our challenges, we can consciously choose to create a healthier future for ourselves and our families. The chapters ahead will equip you with tools and techniques to cultivate self- awareness, improve communication, and manage conflict effectively.

We'll delve into practical strategies for emotional regulation, building resilience, and fostering a secure and loving family environment. Through relatable narratives, research-based insights, and actionable exercises, you will learn how to identify your own trauma triggers, process unresolved emotions, and develop healthier coping mechanisms.

This is a journey of self-discovery and growth, not a quick fix. Embrace the process, be kind to yourself, and remember that creating a healthier family dynamic is an ongoing commitment that yields profound rewards, benefitting both you and the generations to come.

Chapter 1

The Intergenerational Transmission of Trauma

The insidious nature of trauma extends far beyond the individual who experiences it. Its reach stretches across generations, leaving an indelible mark on families and shaping the lives of those who never directly witnessed the original event. This intergenerational transmission of trauma is a complex phenomenon, impacting individuals biologically, psychologically, and behaviorally.

Understanding this process is crucial to breaking the cycle and fostering healthier family dynamics.

One of the key mechanisms through which trauma is passed down is through epigenetics. Epigenetics refers to heritable changes in gene expression that do not involve alterations to the underlying DNA sequence. Essentially, experiences, including traumatic ones, can leave chemical markers on our genes that affect how they are expressed. These markers can be passed down through generations, influencing the susceptibility of offspring to certain mental health conditions, such as anxiety, depression, and PTSD. For example, studies have shown that children of parents who experienced trauma during war or natural disasters have a higher risk of developing these conditions, even if they themselves have not experienced a traumatic event. The implications are profound; a grandparent's experience of war can influence the emotional regulation of their grandchild several generations later.

The psychological impact of intergenerational trauma is equally significant. Unresolved trauma in parents can significantly alter their parenting styles. Parents who experienced neglect or abuse may unknowingly replicate these patterns with their own children, perpetuating a cycle

of harm. They might struggle with emotional regulation, exhibiting anger, irritability, or withdrawal, creating an unpredictable and potentially unsafe environment for their children. This unpredictable environment leads to an increased risk of attachment disorders and emotional instability in the child, which can then manifest as challenges in their own relationships and parenting styles later in life. The effects extend beyond direct interactions; children may learn maladaptive coping mechanisms from observing their parents' struggles, adopting similar strategies to manage stress and emotional distress. These can include substance abuse, self-harm, or avoidance.

The behavioral manifestations of intergenerational trauma are often subtle but pervasive. Individuals may experience heightened anxiety or reactivity to perceived threats, even in seemingly innocuous situations. This can manifest as hypervigilance, difficulty relaxing, or an overreaction to minor stressors. This heightened anxiety and reactivity can impact various aspects of life, from personal relationships to professional success. There can also be difficulties with forming and maintaining healthy relationships, due to learned patterns of distrust, avoidance, or unhealthy dependency, all stemming from the transmitted trauma. The impact on self-esteem can also be significant, with individuals struggling to feel worthy or capable due to inherited patterns of self-criticism and negative self- perception. In essence, the behavioral echoes of past trauma reverberate through families, shaping their behaviors, relationships, and overall well-being.

Beyond the direct impact on parenting styles, the intergenerational transmission of trauma can also affect family narratives and communication patterns. Families who have experienced significant trauma may avoid discussing painful events, creating a culture of silence and secrecy. This

lack of open communication can inhibit emotional processing and healing, leading to a perpetuation of trauma across generations. Conversely, the constant revisiting of traumatic events, even unintentionally, can also be harmful, creating an environment of perpetual anxiety and distress for subsequent generations. Striking a balance between acknowledgement and healthy processing is a vital step toward breaking this cycle.

The subtle ways trauma manifests can make it difficult to identify. It doesn't always present as overt symptoms of PTSD or other clinically diagnosed conditions. Instead, it might be reflected in seemingly minor behaviors, such as an intense fear of abandonment, an inability to trust others, or a constant need for control. It could be seen in the difficulty in forming healthy emotional connections, or a persistent sense of unease and distrust. These less obvious signs are frequently overlooked, making early intervention and family healing particularly challenging. This makes it imperative for both parents and children to be aware of these subtle clues, to seek professional guidance if needed, and to work together toward healing.

Research continues to explore the intricate connections between trauma and genetics, uncovering more complex mechanisms underlying this intergenerational transmission. These studies add significant weight to the understanding that trauma is not simply a personal burden but a family legacy, affecting multiple members across generations. The findings highlight the importance of early intervention and therapeutic approaches that focus not only on the individual but also on the family system as a whole.

Considering the far-reaching consequences of intergenerational trauma, breaking the cycle is not merely desirable; it's vital for the well-being of families and future

generations. This involves a multifaceted approach that encompasses individual healing, improved communication patterns, and conscious efforts to foster healthier family dynamics. It demands a deep understanding of one's own trauma, an acknowledgment of the impact it has on relationships, and a commitment to fostering self-awareness, emotional regulation, and healthy coping mechanisms.

A crucial first step is acknowledging the presence of trauma in the family system. This involves open and honest conversations, potentially with the help of a therapist, to identify past trauma and its current manifestations. Once trauma is acknowledged, individual healing can begin, allowing affected individuals to process their emotions, develop healthy coping strategies, and break free from the shackles of the past. This process involves addressing the emotional pain and psychological wounds caused by past trauma. This can include various therapeutic interventions, such as psychotherapy, trauma-informed therapy, and EMDR (Eye Movement Desensitization and Reprocessing), all geared toward healing emotional wounds and rebuilding mental well-being.

Addressing the impact of trauma on parenting styles is equally critical. Parents who have experienced trauma may unconsciously replicate their own negative experiences in their interactions with their children. Therapy and self- reflection can help parents identify these patterns and develop more mindful and constructive ways of interacting with their children. Learning techniques for emotional regulation, active listening, and setting healthy boundaries are key steps in this process. It's about consciously choosing a different path, breaking the chain of repetition, and creating a more nurturing and secure environment for their children.

Promoting open communication within the family is another essential step towards breaking the cycle. Families affected by intergenerational trauma often struggle with open communication, due to feelings of shame, fear, or guilt associated with past events. Creating a safe space for open dialogue, where family members can share their experiences and emotions without judgment, is essential for healing and fostering healthier family dynamics. This might involve family therapy, where a therapist helps family members improve communication and understand each other's perspectives, working collaboratively to address family conflicts and overcome communication barriers.

Finally, fostering resilience within the family is paramount in disrupting the cycle of trauma. Resilience is the ability to bounce back from adversity and build strength in the face of challenges. By fostering emotional resilience in both parents and children, families become better equipped to cope with life's inevitable stressors and prevent the negative impact of trauma from carrying over into future generations. This involves teaching healthy coping mechanisms, promoting self-esteem, and creating a family environment that emphasizes support, empathy, and connection. It is about building a family narrative that emphasizes hope and resilience, rather than one steeped in fear and negativity.

The intergenerational transmission of trauma is a complex and pervasive phenomenon, but it is not insurmountable. Through conscious effort, self-awareness, and potentially professional guidance, families can break the cycle and create a healthier future for themselves and generations to come. The path to healing is not always easy, but it is achievable. By understanding the intricacies of trauma transmission and actively working towards healing, families can build stronger, healthier relationships and create a legacy of well-being for generations to come. The journey towards

healing is a process of reclaiming one's narrative, shifting family dynamics, and cultivating a sense of hope and resilience. It's a process that requires patience, self- compassion, and unwavering commitment to fostering a healthier family system. But the rewards – a family strengthened by shared healing, resilience, and a future free from the weight of the past – are immeasurable.

Chapter 2

Recognizing the Signs of Trauma in Families

Recognizing the insidious nature of intergenerational trauma requires a keen eye for subtle yet pervasive patterns within family dynamics. These patterns often manifest as unhealthy communication styles, difficulties with emotional regulation, and persistent challenges in forming and maintaining healthy relationships. Understanding these manifestations is crucial to disrupting the cycle and fostering healthier family interactions.

One of the most prominent indicators of trauma's impact is the presence of unhealthy communication patterns. This might involve consistent conflict, characterized by yelling, name-calling, or the use of silence as a weapon. Families grappling with unresolved trauma often struggle with clear, direct, and respectful communication, resorting instead to passive-aggressive behaviors, indirect accusations, or an inability to express needs effectively. Conversations might be laced with criticism, judgment, or an overwhelming sense of defensiveness, hindering genuine connection and understanding. The absence of open and honest dialogue creates a breeding ground for misunderstandings and resentment, ultimately eroding the foundation of healthy family relationships. For instance, a parent who experienced emotional neglect in childhood might struggle to provide emotional support to their own children, resulting in a pervasive sense of emotional unavailability within the family. Conversely, a parent who survived a traumatic event might inadvertently overprotect their children, hindering their development of independence and resilience. This pattern of overprotective parenting can be just as detrimental to a child's emotional well-being as neglect.

Another crucial sign is emotional dysregulation – the inability to manage and express emotions in a healthy manner. This can manifest in various ways, ranging from explosive outbursts of anger and frustration to chronic emotional numbness and detachment. Individuals burdened by intergenerational trauma might struggle to identify and label their emotions, leading to impulsive behaviors and difficulty in regulating their responses to everyday stressors. This difficulty might stem from a lack of emotional modeling during their upbringing, or a learned avoidance of expressing emotions due to past experiences of emotional invalidation or punishment. This can lead to an environment where expressing vulnerability is discouraged and emotional needs are unmet, creating a cycle of emotional suppression and reactivity across generations. For example, children witnessing frequent parental conflict might develop heightened anxiety and difficulty managing their own emotions, mirroring the volatile emotional landscape they have experienced at home. They might exhibit behavioral problems, struggle with academic performance, or engage in self-destructive behaviors as a way of coping with the emotional turmoil they are experiencing. On the other hand, parents who suppress their emotions might appear calm and collected on the surface but struggle with underlying issues of depression, anxiety, or post-traumatic stress disorder, impacting their ability to provide consistent emotional support and guidance to their children. This lack of emotional availability creates a ripple effect within the family, making it difficult for children to develop healthy emotional regulation skills.

The impact of intergenerational trauma is also clearly evident in the difficulties families face in establishing and maintaining healthy relationships. This can manifest as an inability to form secure attachments, difficulties with trust, and persistent patterns of conflict and estrangement.

Individuals who have experienced relational trauma might struggle to form close bonds, exhibiting fear of intimacy or engaging in manipulative behaviors in relationships. They may find it challenging to establish clear boundaries, either becoming overly enmeshed with others or maintaining excessive emotional distance. This pattern often repeats itself across generations, creating a legacy of strained relationships and dysfunctional family dynamics. For instance, a parent with attachment issues might struggle to provide consistent emotional support and affection to their children, leading to insecure attachment styles in the next generation. Children who grow up in an environment where their emotional needs are not met may develop a deep-seated sense of insecurity and difficulty in forming meaningful relationships throughout their lives. Furthermore, the fear of vulnerability stemming from past trauma can lead to a lack of trust in others, making it challenging to form genuine and lasting relationships. This fear can also lead to avoidance of conflict or difficulty in resolving disagreements healthily, perpetuating a cycle of unresolved conflict within the family.

The impact of trauma on parenting styles is profound and multifaceted. Parents who have experienced unresolved trauma often inadvertently replicate unhealthy patterns from their own upbringing, passing these patterns on to their children. This might involve employing harsh disciplinary techniques, emotionally neglecting their children, or engaging in controlling behaviors. Such parenting styles can have devastating effects on children's emotional and psychological well-being, leading to increased risk of anxiety, depression, and other mental health issues. For instance, a parent who experienced physical abuse as a child might resort to physical punishment when disciplining their own children, believing it to be an effective or even necessary approach. This cycle of violence perpetuates trauma across generations, with devastating consequences

for both parents and children. Similarly, parents who suffered from emotional neglect might struggle to express affection or provide emotional support to their children, unintentionally creating a climate of emotional distance and insecurity within the family. This emotional unavailability can lead to children developing insecure attachment styles, affecting their ability to form healthy relationships later in life. These parents, often unknowingly, are re-enacting their own childhood experiences, perpetuating the cycle of trauma.

Conversely, a parent who experienced trauma might adopt an overly permissive parenting style, struggling to set healthy boundaries or enforce appropriate discipline. This might stem from a desire to protect their children from the pain they themselves experienced, but it can ultimately have negative repercussions. Children who lack clear boundaries and consistent guidance may struggle to develop self- discipline, emotional regulation skills, and the ability to navigate the complexities of social interactions. Ultimately, they may struggle to take responsibility for their actions and build healthy relationships. Trauma's influence on parenting is complex and nuanced. It can manifest in various ways, each with unique consequences for the child's development and well-being. Recognizing these variations is crucial in understanding and addressing the intricate interplay between trauma and parenting styles.

Identifying these signs requires careful observation and a willingness to acknowledge the potential impact of past experiences on present-day family dynamics. It is vital to remember that these patterns are not indicative of personal failings or deliberate choices but rather reflections of the enduring effects of trauma. By understanding the mechanisms of intergenerational trauma and recognizing its subtle manifestations, families can begin the process of

healing and breaking free from the cycle of pain and dysfunction. This process requires empathy, self-awareness, and a commitment to fostering healthier communication, emotional regulation, and relational patterns. Seeking professional guidance from therapists specializing in trauma and intergenerational relationships can be instrumental in navigating this complex journey towards healing and building stronger, healthier family connections. The path toward healing is not easy, but it is certainly achievable, leading to a more resilient and loving family system. The commitment to understanding and addressing these signs represents a crucial first step in breaking the cycle of intergenerational trauma and fostering a future where families are empowered to thrive, free from the burden of the past.

Chapter 3

A Path to Healing

Breaking the cycle of generational trauma is not a passive endeavor; it requires conscious effort, a willingness to confront difficult truths, and a commitment to proactive strategies. This journey begins with self-awareness – a deep understanding of one's own emotional landscape, the patterns of behavior inherited from previous generations, and the ways in which those patterns manifest in current relationships, particularly with children. This self-reflection is not about self-blame; rather, it's about recognizing the impact of the past without letting it dictate the present and future. Mindful parenting emerges as a powerful tool in this process. It involves cultivating a present-moment awareness of one's emotions and reactions, allowing for conscious choices in how we respond to our children's needs and behaviors. Instead of reacting automatically based on ingrained patterns, mindful parenting encourages a thoughtful, compassionate approach that prioritizes understanding and connection over judgment and reactivity. This shift requires consistent practice and patience, but the payoff—a healthier, more resilient family—is immeasurable.

The path toward mindful parenting begins with acknowledging the existence of intergenerational trauma within the family system. This acknowledgment is not a confession of failure, but rather a crucial first step in creating a space for healing. It

19

involves examining family history, exploring past traumas, and understanding how those traumas might have impacted parenting styles and family dynamics across generations. This exploration isn't about assigning blame; rather, it's about recognizing the ripple effects of trauma and acknowledging its pervasive influence. For instance, a parent who experienced childhood neglect

might unintentionally replicate that neglect in their own parenting, unaware of the unconscious patterns at play. Recognizing this dynamic is crucial for interrupting the cycle. This introspection can be deeply challenging, requiring individuals to confront difficult emotions and potentially painful memories. It's a process best undertaken with the support of a therapist or support group specifically trained in intergenerational trauma, providing a safe and guided environment to explore these complex issues.

Self-compassion is also a vital component of this journey. Healing from intergenerational trauma is not a sprint; it's a marathon requiring patience, self-forgiveness, and a compassionate understanding of one's limitations.

Individuals must acknowledge that they are not solely responsible for the traumas of their ancestors, yet they bear the responsibility of choosing a different path for themselves and their children. This involves accepting imperfections, acknowledging mistakes, and learning from them without self-criticism. Self-compassion allows for the development of emotional regulation skills, enabling individuals to manage their emotional responses effectively, reducing the likelihood of repeating unhealthy patterns. Practicing mindfulness techniques, such as meditation or deep breathing exercises, can significantly enhance emotional regulation and self-compassion. These practices create space for self-reflection, fostering a greater understanding of one's own emotional triggers and responses.

By developing these skills, parents can better manage stress, regulate their emotions, and create a more stable and nurturing environment for their children.

Building healthy boundaries is another critical aspect of breaking the cycle. Many families struggling with intergenerational trauma have blurred boundaries, leading to codependency, enmeshment, and difficulty establishing

healthy relationships. Establishing clear and healthy boundaries involves setting limits on acceptable behavior, respecting personal space, and prioritizing individual needs without guilt or shame. This requires assertive communication, the ability to say "no" without feeling guilty, and a willingness to protect one's own emotional and physical well-being. For example, a parent who consistently prioritizes the needs of their child at the expense of their own well-being might be unknowingly perpetuating a cycle of neglect or enabling unhealthy behaviors. Learning to set boundaries allows for a healthier balance in the parent-child relationship, creating a space for mutual respect and emotional independence. This process can be challenging, particularly for those who have grown up in families where boundaries were not clearly defined or respected. Seeking professional guidance from a therapist or counselor can be invaluable in learning to establish and maintain healthy boundaries.

Healthy communication is the cornerstone of any strong and healthy relationship, particularly within the family unit. In families impacted by intergenerational trauma, communication patterns can be distorted, characterized by passive-aggressiveness, avoidance, or emotionally charged interactions. Cultivating healthy communication involves practicing active listening, expressing feelings assertively but respectfully, and focusing on empathy and understanding. This requires conscious effort and practice.

For example, instead of resorting to criticism or blame, parents can learn to express concerns using "I" statements, focusing on their own feelings and needs without judging or attacking the child. Active listening involves paying close attention to the child's words, body language, and emotional tone, ensuring that their message is fully understood.

Engaging in family therapy can be especially helpful in improving communication patterns, providing a neutral

space for family members to learn and practice healthy communication skills. Through guided discussions and therapeutic interventions, families can work towards resolving conflicts constructively, fostering mutual respect, and building stronger connections.

Emotional regulation plays a pivotal role in breaking the cycle of generational trauma. Unresolved trauma often manifests as difficulty managing emotions, leading to outbursts of anger, anxiety, or depression. Parents struggling with emotional dysregulation may unintentionally project their emotions onto their children, creating a volatile and unpredictable home environment. Learning to regulate emotions involves developing self-awareness, identifying triggers, and adopting healthy coping mechanisms. This might involve engaging in mindfulness practices, journaling, or seeking support from a therapist. By managing their own emotions effectively, parents can create a more stable and predictable environment for their children, fostering a sense of security and emotional safety. Modeling healthy emotional regulation for children is also crucial; children learn by observing their parents' behavior, and witnessing healthy emotional coping strategies can help them develop their own skills. Providing children with a safe space to express their feelings without judgment is critical, enabling them to build their emotional intelligence and resilience.

Forgiveness, both of oneself and others, is a powerful catalyst for healing. Holding onto resentment and anger related to past traumas can perpetuate cycles of pain and dysfunction. Forgiveness does not mean condoning harmful actions; rather, it involves releasing the burden of negativity and allowing oneself to move forward. This can be a challenging process, often requiring professional guidance. Forgiving oneself for mistakes or perceived failures in parenting is essential, allowing for self-compassion and the

ability to learn from past experiences. Forgiving family members for past hurts can also be transformative, releasing the grip of the past and opening up the possibility of healthier relationships. This process takes time and may require multiple attempts; it's not a linear process, but one that involves repeated cycles of self-reflection and willingness to let go of the burden of negativity. Support groups, spiritual practices, and individual therapy can all offer valuable support in this journey towards forgiveness.

Seeking professional help is not a sign of weakness but a testament to one's commitment to breaking the cycle of generational trauma. Therapists specializing in trauma and intergenerational relationships offer invaluable support, providing a safe space for individuals and families to explore their experiences, develop coping strategies, and learn healthier ways of relating to one another. Therapy can provide tools for emotional regulation, communication enhancement, boundary setting, and forgiveness. Family therapy offers a structured environment for family members to engage in guided discussions, resolving conflicts constructively and fostering mutual understanding.

Individual therapy allows individuals to process their own experiences in a safe and non-judgmental setting, fostering self-awareness and developing healthy coping mechanisms.

Choosing a therapist with expertise in trauma and intergenerational relationships is crucial, as this specialized knowledge is essential for navigating the complexities of these issues effectively. It's crucial to find a therapist that you feel comfortable with, fostering a strong therapeutic alliance to ensure success in the healing process.

Ultimately, breaking the cycle of generational trauma is a journey, not a destination. It requires consistent effort, self-compassion, and a willingness to confront difficult truths. By cultivating self-awareness, practicing mindful parenting,

setting healthy boundaries, improving communication, and fostering emotional regulation, families can begin to heal from the wounds of the past and create a more loving and supportive environment for future generations. Seeking professional help and embracing forgiveness are essential components of this transformative journey. The path toward healing is not easy, but the rewards—a more resilient, connected, and loving family—make it a worthwhile endeavor. The long-term benefits extend beyond the immediate family, creating a ripple effect of healing and empowering future generations to break free from the chains of intergenerational trauma, fostering a legacy of well-being and resilience. The process demands patience, unwavering commitment, and understanding that setbacks are inevitable, yet part of a broader journey toward profound transformation and healing.

Chapter 4

The Importance of SelfCompassion

The journey of healing from generational trauma and fostering healthier parent-child relationships hinges significantly on cultivating self-compassion. This isn't merely a feel-good concept; it's a fundamental cornerstone for breaking free from the cycle of inherited pain. For generations, families have unknowingly carried the burden of unresolved trauma, manifesting as dysfunctional communication patterns, emotional dysregulation, and strained relationships. These patterns often perpetuate a cycle of self-criticism and shame, hindering the ability to connect authentically with oneself and others. The critical inner voice, often fueled by past experiences and inherited beliefs, becomes a formidable obstacle to healing and growth. This inner critic judges harshly, preventing individuals from acknowledging their inherent worthiness and accepting their imperfections. This self-criticism can manifest in various ways, from chronic self-doubt and negative self-talk to perfectionism and an inability to forgive oneself for past mistakes or perceived failings. In the context of parenting, this can translate into unrealistic expectations, harsh judgments of oneself and one's children, and a struggle to provide the nurturing and empathetic environment a child needs to thrive.

The impact of self-criticism and shame extends far beyond individual struggles; it permeates family dynamics, significantly impacting the parent-child relationship. Parents burdened by self-criticism often struggle to offer unconditional love and acceptance to their children, mirroring the lack of compassion they experienced or internalized during their own upbringing. Children, in turn, internalize these patterns, absorbing the negativity and

developing their own critical inner voices. This cycle perpetuates the generational transmission of trauma, hindering the development of healthy self-esteem and emotional well-being across generations. A parent grappling with their own unresolved trauma and lacking self- compassion may inadvertently project their pain onto their children, creating a climate of fear, anxiety, and emotional insecurity. Children raised in such environments may develop coping mechanisms like avoidance, people-pleasing, or aggression, further complicating their relationships with their caregivers and perpetuating the cycle of trauma.

Self-compassion, therefore, emerges as a vital antidote to this destructive pattern. It involves treating oneself with the same kindness, understanding, and acceptance that one would offer a dear friend struggling with similar challenges. It's about recognizing that everyone makes mistakes, experiences setbacks, and faces moments of vulnerability.

Instead of dwelling on imperfections and engaging in self-criticism, self-compassion encourages self-acceptance and a willingness to learn from past experiences without succumbing to self-judgment. This isn't about self- indulgence or a lack of accountability; rather, it's about fostering a healthy relationship with oneself, acknowledging one's strengths and weaknesses with empathy and understanding. A crucial aspect of self-compassion involves recognizing that suffering is a shared human experience.

Acknowledging that we are not alone in our struggles fosters a sense of connection and reduces feelings of isolation and shame.

Cultivating self-compassion is an ongoing process, requiring conscious effort and mindful practice. One effective method involves practicing self-soothing techniques. This might involve engaging in activities that bring comfort and relaxation, such as listening to calming music, spending time

in nature, practicing mindfulness meditation, or engaging in hobbies that promote a sense of peace and well-being.

Mindfulness practices, in particular, are exceptionally valuable in developing self-compassion. By bringing awareness to our thoughts and emotions without judgment, we create space to observe our inner critic without being consumed by it. This creates an opportunity to respond to negative thoughts with kindness and self-acceptance rather than harsh judgment.

Another crucial aspect of self-compassion involves reframing negative self-talk. This involves challenging negative thoughts and replacing them with more balanced and compassionate ones. For example, instead of dwelling on a mistake, one might acknowledge the imperfection and focus on learning from the experience. Instead of judging oneself harshly for feeling overwhelmed, one might acknowledge the validity of their emotions and offer oneself comfort and understanding. This process requires patience and practice, as ingrained negative patterns of thought can be deeply entrenched. Journaling can be a powerful tool in this process, providing a space to explore one's thoughts and emotions without judgment and fostering self-awareness.

Through consistent journaling, one can identify recurring negative thought patterns, challenge their validity, and gradually replace them with more self-compassionate and balanced ones.

Moreover, practicing gratitude is a profoundly effective method for cultivating self-compassion. By focusing on the positive aspects of one's life, even during challenging times, we shift our perspective and nurture a sense of appreciation for ourselves and the world around us. This doesn't mean ignoring difficult emotions; rather, it involves acknowledging both the positive and negative aspects of our experiences, recognizing that even during hardship, there are

aspects of our lives for which we can be grateful. Regularly listing things we're thankful for—be it personal accomplishments, supportive relationships, or simple joys— can significantly shift our mindset and foster a sense of self- worth.

Beyond personal practices, seeking professional support plays a pivotal role in fostering self-compassion. A therapist can provide guidance and support in identifying and challenging negative thought patterns, developing healthier coping mechanisms, and fostering self-acceptance. Therapy provides a safe and non-judgmental space to explore past traumas and their impact on one's self-perception. It facilitates the development of self-awareness and helps individuals recognize the origins of their self-criticism, empowering them to break free from the cycle of self- judgment and cultivate self-compassion. Therapy can also provide tools for improving communication skills, setting healthy boundaries, and fostering healthier relationships with oneself and others. Through therapeutic interventions, individuals can learn to manage their emotions more effectively, reducing the impact of past trauma on their present-day lives and fostering healthier family dynamics.

The journey toward self-compassion is not a linear one; it involves ups and downs, setbacks, and moments of self- doubt. It's crucial to approach this process with kindness and patience, recognizing that it's a journey of self-discovery and growth. Self-compassion isn't a destination but a continuous process of self-acceptance, self-understanding, and self-care. It's a commitment to treating oneself with the same kindness, empathy, and understanding that one would offer a cherished friend or family member facing similar challenges. By embracing self-compassion, parents can create a safer, more nurturing environment for their children, breaking free from the cycle of generational trauma and fostering healthier

family relationships. The impact extends beyond the immediate family, rippling outwards to future generations, creating a legacy of resilience, self-acceptance, and emotional well-being. The ripple effect of a parent's journey towards self-compassion can transform not only their relationship with their children but also their own lives and the lives of generations to come, cultivating a family culture built on empathy, understanding, and genuine connection.

The power of self-compassion lies in its ability to foster healing, resilience, and ultimately, a brighter future for the entire family.

Chapter 5

Seeking Professional Support

The journey towards healing from generational trauma is deeply personal and often challenging. While self- compassion and conscious effort are vital, recognizing when professional support is necessary is equally important. The impact of unresolved trauma can be insidious, manifesting in various ways that may not be immediately apparent.

Persistent negative emotional patterns, such as chronic anxiety, depression, overwhelming anger, or difficulty regulating emotions, can significantly impact your ability to parent effectively and build healthy relationships. These are clear signals that seeking professional guidance might be beneficial. Furthermore, if you find yourself struggling with repetitive, destructive patterns in your relationships, particularly with your children, it's a sign that professional intervention can provide valuable tools and insights. This could include difficulties setting boundaries, consistent conflict, or feeling overwhelmed by the emotional demands of parenting. If your attempts at self-help and improving communication haven't yielded significant progress, professional support can offer a structured and personalized approach to address the root causes of your challenges. Early intervention is crucial; addressing these issues early can prevent the perpetuation of these patterns to future generations. Delaying help can allow these deeply ingrained issues to take root more firmly, making the healing process more complex and potentially longer.

The types of therapy that can be particularly beneficial in addressing generational trauma and improving parent-child relationships are varied and often used in combination.

Trauma-informed therapy is essential. This approach recognizes the profound impact of trauma on individuals and

families, providing a safe and supportive environment to explore past experiences without re-traumatization.

Therapists trained in this modality understand the unique complexities of trauma and employ techniques designed to help clients process their experiences in a way that fosters healing and resilience. Techniques such as EMDR (Eye Movement Desensitization and Reprocessing) are frequently used to help process traumatic memories and reduce their emotional impact. EMDR is particularly effective in addressing the lingering effects of past trauma on present- day functioning. Another valuable approach is family systems therapy, which focuses on the interconnectedness of family members and how their interactions contribute to the overall family dynamic. This approach explores how unresolved conflicts and patterns of interaction have been passed down through generations and contribute to current relationship challenges. Family systems therapists work with families to identify these patterns and develop healthier communication and interaction styles, fostering greater understanding and improved emotional regulation within the family unit. Cognitive Behavioral Therapy (CBT) can be helpful in identifying and modifying negative thought patterns and behaviors that perpetuate the cycle of trauma.

CBT teaches individuals to challenge their negative beliefs, develop healthier coping mechanisms, and build more adaptive behaviors. This is particularly useful in addressing anxieties, fears, and emotional dysregulation often associated with unresolved trauma. Finally, attachment- based therapy offers a deeper exploration of the parent-child relationship and its connection to past experiences. This type of therapy focuses on understanding and repairing attachment wounds that can stem from past trauma. It helps parents develop secure attachment patterns with their children, leading to more loving, supportive, and emotionally healthy relationships.

Finding a suitable therapist requires careful consideration and research. Begin by identifying your specific needs and goals for therapy. Do you want to address individual trauma, improve your parenting skills, or work on family dynamics? Clarifying your needs will help you focus your search. Then, explore therapist directories, such as Psychology Today's therapist finder or your insurance company's provider network. Read reviews and testimonials to get a sense of other clients' experiences. When you identify potential therapists, carefully review their qualifications and experience. Make sure that they have expertise in trauma- informed therapy, family systems therapy, or other relevant approaches. It's important to find a therapist who is a good fit for you personally; someone with whom you feel comfortable, safe, and understood. The therapeutic relationship is a crucial element of successful therapy.

Schedule an initial consultation or phone call with a few therapists to discuss your needs and their approach. This will allow you to assess the therapist's style and determine if it aligns with your preferences and treatment goals. Don't hesitate to ask questions. A good therapist will be transparent about their approach and be happy to answer your questions. Building rapport and trust with your therapist is paramount for successful treatment; the comfort level you feel with them is as vital as the theoretical approaches they employ. The goal is to create a space where you can safely explore painful experiences and work towards healing without judgment.

The cost of therapy can vary considerably depending on the therapist's location, experience, and the type of insurance coverage you have. Many therapists offer sliding-scale fees to accommodate clients with limited financial resources.

Explore your options carefully, including your insurance coverage, and determine how you can comfortably afford the cost of therapy. It's crucial to prioritize your mental health

and well-being, and finding a therapist you can financially afford should be part of the search. Remember, investing in your mental health is investing in your family's well-being. Don't underestimate the long-term benefits of healing from generational trauma. The effects of resolving past trauma, improving communication, and fostering healthier family dynamics are immeasurable. The cost is a short-term investment for a profound, long-term impact on your life and the lives of future generations.

Beyond the practical aspects of finding a therapist, remember that seeking professional help is a sign of strength, not weakness. It takes courage to confront difficult experiences and seek help in healing. Many people harbor misconceptions about therapy, viewing it as a sign of failure or inability to cope. However, therapy is a proactive step toward self-improvement and building healthier relationships. It's a tool to enhance your ability to navigate life's challenges and foster resilience within yourself and your family. Acknowledge your own strength and courage in recognizing the need for professional support and actively taking steps to address the issues that affect you and your family. Remember that you're not alone; many families face similar struggles, and seeking help is a pathway towards a brighter future. This journey may have its challenges, and setbacks are normal, but with perseverance and the support of a skilled therapist, you can build healthier relationships and break free from the cycles of trauma that have impacted your family for generations.

The process of healing from generational trauma requires a commitment to understanding its complex influence on your life and family dynamics. It's not a quick fix; rather, it's a journey of self-discovery, personal growth, and relationship building. This involves ongoing self-reflection, honest communication within the family, and a proactive approach

to addressing emotional challenges. Throughout this process, remember the importance of self-compassion, patience, and understanding. Be kind to yourself as you navigate the complexities of your experiences and the impact they've had on your family. Progress is not always linear, and setbacks are part of the process. Acknowledge those setbacks without judgment or self-criticism; instead, use them as opportunities for learning and growth. Celebrate your successes, no matter how small, and maintain a focus on the overall goals you've set for your family's well-being. This journey is not just about addressing past hurts; it's about building a stronger, healthier future for yourself and your loved ones. It is about creating a legacy of healing and resilience that will positively impact future generations.

Remember that you are not alone in this journey. Many families have successfully navigated similar challenges with the support of professionals and a steadfast commitment to growth. The path to healing might be long and winding, but the destination – a more loving, connected, and emotionally healthy family – is worth the effort. This journey is about fostering a future where your children can thrive, free from the weight of inherited trauma, empowered to build their own resilient and fulfilling lives. The investment in your family's well-being is an investment in their future, a gift that extends beyond your lifetime and helps create a legacy of strength and well-being for generations to come. As you embark on this journey of healing and growth, remember that every step you take, every challenge you overcome, is a testament to your resilience and your commitment to building a healthier and happier future for your family.

Celebrate these steps and milestones along the way; they mark significant progress toward a brighter future. With dedication and unwavering support, you can create a family culture built on empathy, understanding, and genuine connection – a legacy you will be proud to pass on.

Chapter 6

Identifying Your Personal Trauma Triggers

Understanding your personal trauma triggers is a crucial first step towards healing and building healthier relationships with your children. Many of us navigate life unknowingly reacting to past traumas, often manifesting as difficulties in parenting. These reactions can range from seemingly minor irritations escalating into disproportionate anger to feeling overwhelmed by simple tasks. Identifying these triggers allows us to understand the root of our responses, fostering self-compassion and paving the way for more mindful interactions. The process isn't always easy; it requires introspection, patience, and potentially professional guidance. But the rewards – a more peaceful and loving relationship with yourself and your children – are immeasurable.

One effective method for identifying triggers is through mindful self-observation. This involves paying close attention to your thoughts, feelings, and physical sensations throughout the day. Notice any patterns emerging. Do you feel a surge of anxiety or anger when your child makes a certain noise, or when they exhibit a particular behavior? Do specific situations, such as deadlines, family gatherings, or even the sight of certain objects, evoke strong emotional responses? Keep a journal to document these instances.

Record the event, your immediate physical and emotional reactions (e.g., racing heart, shortness of breath, anger, sadness, fear), and any thoughts or memories that surfaced.

Over time, you might begin to notice recurring themes. Perhaps loud noises trigger flashbacks to a childhood incident involving a frightening experience. Or perhaps the smell of a specific perfume reminds you of a past

relationship that caused significant emotional pain. These seemingly insignificant occurrences might actually be triggers, tapping into deeply ingrained memories and emotional responses. It's crucial to remember that there is no right or wrong way to feel in response to a trigger.

Recognizing the emotional response is the first critical step.

Another useful technique is to explore your past experiences. While revisiting painful memories isn't always enjoyable, it can provide invaluable insight into your present-day reactions. Consider childhood experiences, significant relationships, and any events that left you feeling unsafe, betrayed, or deeply hurt. Think about how those experiences might be shaping your current beliefs and behaviors.

Therapy can be particularly helpful in this process, providing a safe and supportive environment to process these memories with a trained professional.

For example, a parent struggling with anger towards their child's messy room might find their reaction linked to a history of feeling neglected or unvalued as a child. The messiness might trigger feelings of abandonment or invalidation, leading to an outburst disproportionate to the situation. Recognizing this connection – the trigger (messy room) and the underlying emotion (neglect) – is pivotal.

Understanding this helps to separate the present-day situation from the past trauma, paving the way for a more measured response.

Identifying triggers isn't about assigning blame or dwelling on the past. Instead, it's about gaining a better understanding of yourself and your reactions. By recognizing your triggers, you can begin to anticipate potential challenges and develop coping mechanisms to help you navigate them. This may involve deep breathing exercises, mindfulness practices, or engaging in activities that bring you comfort and calm.

Moreover, consider the physical manifestations of your triggers. Trauma often manifests not only emotionally but also physically. Pay attention to your body's responses. Do you tense your muscles, experience headaches, or feel nauseous when confronted with a trigger? These physical sensations are just as significant as emotional responses.

Learning to recognize these bodily cues can be a powerful tool for preventing escalating reactions. For instance, if you notice your heart racing and muscles tightening when your child is having a tantrum, take a moment to practice deep breathing or step away from the situation to regain composure.

It's vital to approach this process with self-compassion. Healing from trauma takes time, and there will likely be setbacks. Don't beat yourself up for having strong emotional responses. Acknowledge your feelings, validate your experiences, and remember that you're not alone. Many parents struggle with similar challenges. It's a journey of self-discovery and self-acceptance, not a race. Be patient with yourself, and celebrate small victories along the way.

Furthermore, consider exploring the role of attachment styles in your responses to triggers. Your attachment style, developed in early childhood, significantly influences your relationships and reactions to stress. Secure attachment, characterized by trust and emotional availability, allows for healthier responses to challenging situations. Conversely, insecure attachment patterns (anxious-preoccupied, dismissive-avoidant, fearful-avoidant) can intensify reactions to triggers, leading to unhealthy coping mechanisms.

Understanding your attachment style can illuminate the roots of your reactivity and inform strategies for creating more secure connections with your children.

Identifying triggers is an ongoing process, requiring continuous self-reflection and awareness. The more you observe your responses and understand their underlying causes, the more equipped you'll be to respond mindfully rather than reactively. Remember, the goal isn't to eliminate all triggers, but to develop the ability to manage your reactions in healthy ways. This, in turn, will lead to more harmonious and loving relationships with your children.

Consider utilizing various tools and techniques beyond self-observation and journaling. Cognitive Behavioral Therapy (CBT) techniques, for instance, can be very useful in identifying and challenging negative thought patterns associated with triggers. These techniques may involve reframing negative thoughts, replacing them with more realistic and positive ones, and developing coping strategies to manage emotional responses. Mindfulness practices, such as meditation or yoga, can also be extremely beneficial in cultivating self-awareness and regulating emotions. These practices help you to observe your thoughts and feelings without judgment, allowing you to respond to triggers with greater equanimity.

The support of a therapist or counselor specializing in trauma can be invaluable in this process. A therapist can provide a safe and confidential space to explore your past experiences, identify triggers, and develop healthy coping mechanisms. They can also help you process complex emotions and develop strategies to manage challenging situations. Remember, seeking professional help is a sign of strength, not weakness. It demonstrates a commitment to personal growth and to creating healthier relationships with your children.

Another crucial aspect is understanding the role of shame and self-criticism in exacerbating your response to triggers.

Many of us carry unresolved feelings of shame from past experiences. When faced with triggers, these feelings may resurface, leading to self-criticism and negative self-talk. This intensifies the emotional response and may lead to unhealthy coping mechanisms. Learning to challenge these self-critical thoughts and replace them with self-compassion is a crucial step in managing your triggers effectively. This can be achieved through mindfulness practices, positive affirmations, and actively challenging negative self-talk.

Finally, remember that identifying your triggers is just the beginning. It's an important step, a critical foundation, upon which you can build a healthier and more fulfilling relationship with yourself and your children. The knowledge gained from understanding your triggers will empower you to respond to future situations with greater self-awareness, empathy, and understanding. By actively engaging in this process of self-discovery, you can break the cycle of intergenerational trauma and build a legacy of healing for your family. The journey may be challenging, but the reward of a more peaceful, loving, and resilient family is well worth the effort. Embrace the process, be kind to yourself, and celebrate your progress along the way.

Chapter 7

Exploring Unresolved Emotions and Grief

Building upon the understanding of personal trauma triggers, we now delve into the crucial process of addressing unresolved emotions and grief. These often lie dormant, subtly influencing our parenting styles and relationships with our children. Unresolved grief, stemming from loss, betrayal, or even unspoken hurts, can manifest as irritability, anxiety, or an inability to connect emotionally. Similarly, unexpressed anger, fear, or sadness related to past trauma can lead to emotional outbursts, detachment, or overly controlling behaviors towards our children.

The first step involves acknowledging the presence of these unresolved emotions. This isn't about wallowing in negativity, but about recognizing their existence and their potential impact on our lives and our children's well-being. Many of us have learned to suppress or ignore our feelings, often believing that showing vulnerability is a sign of weakness. However, the opposite is true. Ignoring or suppressing these emotions only allows them to fester and manifest in unhealthy ways. For example, a parent who suppressed grief over the loss of a sibling might unconsciously project that sadness onto their child, leading to excessive worry or overprotectiveness. Or a parent who never processed childhood abuse might unknowingly recreate a similar dynamic within their own family, leading to unhealthy power imbalances.

Understanding the connection between unresolved emotions and our parenting styles requires honest self-reflection. This is often challenging, as confronting past traumas can be deeply painful. Journaling can be an invaluable tool in this process. Writing down our thoughts and feelings, without

judgment, allows us to externalize these emotions and gain a clearer perspective. Consider writing about specific memories, noting the emotions they evoke, and identifying any patterns that emerge. For example, you might find that feelings of abandonment resurface whenever your child pushes boundaries or seems distant, triggering intense anxiety or anger. Reflecting on these connections provides valuable insights into our subconscious responses.

Beyond journaling, exploring creative outlets can offer a powerful means of emotional expression. Art therapy, music therapy, or even simply engaging in creative writing can help unlock and process pent-up emotions. The act of creating, whether painting, playing music, or writing poetry, can serve as a cathartic release, enabling us to express feelings that we might struggle to articulate verbally. Consider exploring different mediums until you find one that resonates with you. This process can be particularly powerful for individuals who struggle to verbalize their emotions directly.

While self-exploration is crucial, seeking professional support is equally important. A therapist can provide a safe and non-judgmental space to explore these deep-seated emotions. They can help you process trauma, develop healthy coping mechanisms, and learn to manage triggers. Cognitive Behavioral

Therapy (CBT), for instance, is particularly effective in helping individuals identify and change negative thought patterns that contribute to emotional distress. Eye Movement Desensitization and Reprocessing (EMDR) therapy has also proven highly successful in treating trauma-related symptoms. Don't hesitate to reach out for professional guidance; it's a sign of strength, not weakness, to seek help in navigating these complex emotions.

Furthermore, fostering a strong support system is vital. Connecting with friends, family, or support groups can offer invaluable emotional support and understanding. Sharing your experiences with others who understand can reduce feelings of isolation and shame. Support groups specifically designed for individuals dealing with trauma or grief can be especially helpful, providing a safe space to share experiences and learn from others. Finding a group that aligns with your specific needs can significantly impact your healing journey. Remember, you are not alone in this process.

In addition to professional help and support networks, it's critical to cultivate self-compassion. Be kind to yourself throughout this process. Healing takes time, and there will be setbacks along the way. Acknowledge your progress, no matter how small, and celebrate your successes. Avoid self- criticism and remember that healing is a journey, not a destination. Focus on building self-awareness, understanding your emotional responses, and developing healthier coping strategies.

The concept of emotional expression, often overlooked, deserves significant attention. Healthy emotional expression is not about venting anger or unleashing negativity. Instead, it's about finding appropriate and constructive ways to communicate your feelings. This involves learning to identify your emotions, articulate them clearly and respectfully, and express them in a way that doesn't harm yourself or others. This might involve practicing assertive communication, learning to set healthy boundaries, or seeking professional guidance in managing intense emotions.

For example, if you're feeling overwhelmed by stress and anger, consider engaging in activities like deep breathing exercises, yoga, or meditation. These techniques can help

regulate your nervous system and calm your emotions. If you're feeling sad or grieving, allowing yourself to feel those emotions without judgment is crucial. This could involve talking to a trusted friend or family member, journaling about your feelings, or engaging in creative expression. The key is finding healthy and constructive ways to channel and express your emotions, rather than suppressing them.

Suppression often leads to a build-up of tension and could lead to emotional outbursts later on.

Learning to express emotions effectively requires practice. Start with small steps. Begin by identifying and labeling your emotions. Try saying, "I feel frustrated," or "I feel sad," instead of resorting to generalizations like, "I'm angry" or "Everything is terrible." The more specific you can be with your emotions, the better you'll be able to understand and address them. Then, practice expressing these emotions to a trusted friend or family member. Start with less intense emotions before addressing more sensitive or painful ones.

The goal is to create a safe and supportive environment where you can feel comfortable expressing your emotions without fear of judgment.

Building upon the ability to express your own emotions, actively listening to your children's emotions is equally critical. Creating a family environment where children feel safe to express their feelings without fear of criticism or punishment is fundamental. This requires active listening, validation of their feelings, and avoiding dismissing or minimizing their experiences. When children feel heard and understood, they develop a stronger sense of self-worth and emotional resilience. This fosters healthier communication patterns within the family, breaking the cycle of suppressed emotions.

Consider incorporating family rituals that encourage open communication and emotional expression. Regular family dinners, game nights, or even simply setting aside time for family discussions can create opportunities for sharing feelings and experiences. These rituals establish a sense of safety and connection, making it easier for family members to communicate openly and honestly. These are opportunities to model healthy emotional expression for your children and demonstrate that it's acceptable, even healthy, to feel a wide range of emotions.

Beyond family rituals, remember the power of physical touch. A hug, a comforting hand on the shoulder, or simply sitting close can communicate care and empathy. Physical affection can provide a nonverbal form of emotional support, especially for children who may struggle to articulate their feelings. Physical touch, when appropriate and consensual, can be a powerful way to foster emotional closeness and connection.

Addressing unresolved emotions and grief is a continuous process, not a one-time fix. It requires consistent self- reflection, practice, and ongoing support. By cultivating self- awareness, expressing emotions healthily, and actively seeking support, parents can create a healthier family environment, free from the burden of past trauma. This conscious work breaks the cycle of intergenerational trauma, paving the way for more resilient and emotionally healthy future generations. The journey may be challenging, filled with moments of discomfort and vulnerability, but the reward of a more emotionally connected and supportive family is invaluable. Remember to be patient with yourself, acknowledge your progress, and celebrate your resilience.

The path to healing is paved with small, consistent steps forward.

Chapter 8

Developing Healthy Coping Mechanisms

Building upon the foundation of self-awareness established in the previous section, we now turn our attention to developing healthy coping mechanisms. These are essential tools for navigating the inevitable stresses and emotional challenges that arise in daily life, particularly for parents grappling with the legacy of intergenerational trauma.

Unmanaged stress and anxiety can easily escalate, hindering our ability to parent effectively and nurturing a cycle of unhealthy emotional responses that can be passed down to future generations. The key is to actively cultivate strategies that help us manage these intense emotions in healthy and constructive ways, promoting emotional regulation and resilience.

One of the most effective strategies is mindfulness. Mindfulness involves paying attention to the present moment without judgment. This isn't about emptying your mind; rather, it's about acknowledging your thoughts and feelings without getting swept away by them. Simple mindfulness practices, such as deep breathing exercises, body scans, or mindful walking, can significantly reduce stress levels and promote a sense of calm. Even a few minutes of mindful breathing throughout the day can create a noticeable difference in your emotional state. Start with just five minutes, focusing on the sensation of your breath entering and leaving your body. When your mind wanders (and it will!), gently redirect your attention back to your breath.

Over time, you'll build your ability to observe your thoughts and feelings without becoming entangled in them, allowing you to respond rather than react to challenging situations.

Another powerful coping mechanism is physical activity. Exercise releases endorphins, natural mood boosters that reduce stress and anxiety. It doesn't have to be intense; a brisk walk, a bike ride, or a simple yoga session can be incredibly beneficial. Find an activity you enjoy and make it a regular part of your routine. This could be a daily walk with your child, joining a gym class, or even dancing to your favorite music at home. The goal is to find something that moves your body and lifts your spirits. The positive impact on both your physical and mental well-being will be substantial, contributing to a more balanced and resilient emotional state.

Beyond physical exercise, engaging in activities that bring you joy and a sense of accomplishment is vital. This could be anything from pursuing a hobby, like painting or gardening, to spending time in nature, reading a book, or listening to music. These activities serve as positive distractions from stress and help restore a sense of balance. Making time for these pleasurable activities isn't selfish; it's self-care. By prioritizing activities that nourish your soul, you're investing in your emotional well-being and strengthening your capacity to cope with challenges. This is especially crucial for parents who might feel depleted from the demands of parenting and the ongoing emotional work of addressing intergenerational trauma.

Developing healthy social connections is another crucial aspect of developing robust coping mechanisms. Connecting with supportive friends, family, or a therapist provides a safe space to share your feelings, receive encouragement, and gain perspective. Isolation can amplify stress and anxiety; conversely, social support provides a buffer against emotional distress. Make an effort to nurture your relationships with trusted individuals. This might involve scheduling regular phone calls, arranging get-togethers, or

simply sharing your struggles with someone you trust. Remember, you don't have to carry the burden of intergenerational trauma alone. Leaning on others for support can significantly enhance your ability to manage stress and navigate life's challenges.

Journaling can be a surprisingly effective tool for processing emotions and gaining self-awareness. Writing down your thoughts and feelings, without judgment, can help you identify patterns, understand your triggers, and develop healthier ways of responding to stressful situations.

Journaling doesn't have to be a formal process; it can be as simple as writing a few sentences each day about how you're feeling. The act of putting your feelings into words can help to externalize them, reducing their intensity and making them easier to manage. Over time, you might start to notice recurring themes or patterns in your journal entries, providing valuable insights into your emotional landscape and informing your coping strategies.

Setting healthy boundaries is a fundamental aspect of self-care and emotional well-being. This involves learning to say no to requests that drain your energy or compromise your well-being. Setting boundaries protects your emotional space and helps prevent burnout. This is particularly important for parents who often find themselves prioritizing the needs of others above their own. Learning to assertively communicate your limits and needs is essential for maintaining healthy relationships and avoiding resentment. This might involve saying no to extra commitments, setting aside time for yourself each day, or limiting contact with individuals who are consistently draining or negative.

In addition to the techniques already discussed, seeking professional support is an invaluable step in developing healthy coping mechanisms, particularly when dealing with

the complex dynamics of intergenerational trauma. A therapist specializing in trauma can provide a safe and supportive environment to explore your experiences, process unresolved emotions, and learn healthier coping skills.

Therapy offers a structured framework for understanding the impact of past trauma on your present-day life and developing strategies to manage its effects. This support system can provide tools and techniques to regulate emotions, enhance self-esteem, and break free from harmful patterns. Remember, seeking professional help is a sign of strength, not weakness, and it can significantly improve your ability to heal and thrive.

Moreover, exploring creative outlets can be a powerful way to process emotions and promote emotional regulation.

Engaging in creative pursuits, such as painting, music, writing, or dance, allows for non-verbal expression of feelings that may be difficult to articulate verbally. These activities can provide a healthy release for pent-up emotions, facilitating self-discovery and personal growth. The process of creation itself can be therapeutic, offering a sense of accomplishment and fostering a feeling of self-efficacy. This is especially relevant for individuals who may struggle with verbal processing or find it difficult to express their emotions through traditional therapeutic methods.

Developing healthy sleep habits is also crucial for effective stress management. Sufficient sleep allows for physical and emotional restoration, impacting our mood, energy levels, and cognitive function. A consistent sleep schedule, creating a relaxing bedtime routine, and ensuring a comfortable sleep environment can significantly improve sleep quality.

Adequate sleep is vital for emotional regulation and resilience. When sleep-deprived, we are more susceptible to heightened emotional reactivity and decreased coping abilities. Prioritizing sleep is an act of self-care that enhances

our overall well-being and strengthens our ability to handle stress effectively.

Nutrition plays a significant role in our emotional well- being. A balanced diet provides the essential nutrients our bodies and minds need to function optimally. Regular intake of nutrient-rich foods supports mood regulation, cognitive function, and energy levels. Conversely, a diet lacking in essential nutrients can negatively impact our emotional state, increasing vulnerability to stress and anxiety. By focusing on a balanced and nourishing diet, we are actively investing in our emotional resilience. This involves incorporating a variety of fruits, vegetables, whole grains, and lean proteins into our daily intake. Limiting processed foods, excessive sugar, and caffeine also promotes emotional well-being.

Finally, the practice of self-compassion is paramount. This involves treating ourselves with the same kindness and understanding that we would offer a close friend. It's about acknowledging our imperfections, accepting our vulnerability, and recognizing that making mistakes is a part of the human experience. Self-criticism and self-judgment can exacerbate stress and anxiety, hindering our ability to heal and grow. Cultivating self-compassion allows us to approach challenges with greater empathy and resilience, fostering a positive relationship with ourselves and our emotions. This means acknowledging our struggles, treating ourselves with kindness, and recognizing our inherent worthiness of love and acceptance. It is a conscious choice to focus on self-encouragement and support rather than self- criticism and self-doubt. This mindset shift is transformative in fostering emotional healing and resilience. The journey of developing healthy coping mechanisms is a personal one, requiring patience, self-compassion, and ongoing effort. By incorporating these strategies into our lives, we create a solid foundation for emotional well-being, breaking the cycle of

intergenerational trauma and fostering healthier relationships with ourselves and our children.

Chapter 9

The Power of SelfReflection and Journaling

Building on the development of healthy coping mechanisms, the next crucial step in breaking free from the chains of intergenerational trauma lies in embracing the power of self- reflection and journaling. These practices offer a profound avenue for increased self-awareness, facilitating a deeper understanding of our emotional responses, ingrained patterns, and the subtle ways in which past experiences continue to shape our present-day interactions. While coping mechanisms provide immediate strategies for managing difficult emotions, self-reflection and journaling provide the space for long-term healing and transformation. They allow us to delve into the root causes of our reactions, identifying triggers and developing a more nuanced understanding of our inner landscape. This process is not about dwelling on the negative; rather, it's about gaining clarity, fostering self- compassion, and empowering ourselves to make conscious choices that lead to healthier relationships and a more fulfilling life.

Journaling, in its simplest form, is a conversation with oneself. It's a safe space to explore thoughts and feelings without judgment, allowing for the free flow of emotions without the pressure of immediate solutions. The act of writing itself can be incredibly therapeutic. Putting words to our experiences, both positive and negative, allows us to externalize them, reducing their internal intensity. It offers a tangible record of our emotional journey, allowing us to track our progress over time and celebrate our growth. There is no right or wrong way to journal. Some may find solace in stream-of-consciousness writing, pouring out whatever comes to mind. Others may prefer a more structured approach, focusing on specific themes or prompts, such as

reflecting on daily interactions with our children, identifying patterns in our emotional responses, or exploring recurring thoughts and anxieties.

The benefits extend far beyond mere emotional release. Regular journaling fosters mindfulness, enhancing our ability to be present in the moment and observe our thoughts and feelings without judgment. This heightened awareness allows us to recognize triggers and patterns that might otherwise go unnoticed. For example, consistent journaling might reveal a tendency to react defensively when our children challenge our authority, a pattern that may stem from unresolved childhood experiences with our own parents. Through journaling, we can begin to untangle these complex dynamics, gaining insight into the root causes of our reactions and developing healthier responses. This process of self-discovery can be incredibly empowering, enabling us to break free from ingrained patterns of behavior that perpetuate cycles of intergenerational trauma.

Self-reflection, hand-in-hand with journaling, is the active process of examining our thoughts, feelings, and behaviors. It's about stepping back from our immediate reactions and asking ourselves probing questions: What triggered this emotion? What are my underlying beliefs or assumptions? How did my upbringing influence this response? These reflective questions lead to a deeper understanding of ourselves and our relationships with others. For instance, if a parent finds themselves constantly yelling at their children, self-reflection might unearth underlying feelings of frustration and helplessness, potentially stemming from their own challenging childhood experiences. This understanding allows them to move beyond simply managing the outbursts to addressing the root cause of the anger.

The combination of journaling and self-reflection offers a powerful synergy. Journaling provides a concrete space for documenting our emotional experiences, while self- reflection allows us to analyze and interpret these experiences, gaining deeper insight into our patterns and motivations. It's a cyclical process, where insights gained through reflection inform future journaling entries, leading to a continuously evolving self-awareness. This deeper understanding is crucial for breaking the cycle of intergenerational trauma. By understanding the roots of our emotional responses, we can consciously choose different patterns of behavior, disrupting the cycle and fostering healthier family dynamics.

To illustrate the practical application of these techniques, let's consider a hypothetical scenario. A parent, Sarah, finds herself consistently struggling with her teenage daughter, Emily. Their conflicts often escalate into shouting matches, leaving both feeling hurt and frustrated. Sarah, aware of the potential impact of intergenerational trauma, decides to incorporate journaling and self-reflection into her daily routine. She starts by journaling after each interaction with Emily, documenting the details of the conflict, her emotional response, and any recurring patterns she notices. Through this process, she begins to identify a consistent trigger: Emily's challenging of Sarah's authority.

After several days of journaling, Sarah sits down for a dedicated session of self-reflection. She reviews her journal entries, searching for underlying themes and connections.

She realizes that her intense reactions to Emily's challenges stem from her own upbringing, where expressing dissent to her authoritative parents was met with harsh criticism and punishment. This realization is a pivotal moment. It shifts her perspective from viewing Emily's behavior as a personal attack to recognizing it as a manifestation of normal

adolescent development. It also helps her understand her own emotional responses as stemming from past experiences rather than Emily's current actions.

Armed with this newfound self-awareness, Sarah starts adjusting her approach to conflicts with Emily. Instead of reacting defensively, she practices active listening, trying to understand Emily's perspective before responding. She uses her journaling to track the progress of this new approach, observing changes in her emotional reactions and the overall dynamic of their interactions. This continuous process of journaling, self-reflection, and conscious behavioral change allows Sarah to disrupt the cycle of intergenerational trauma, fostering a healthier and more constructive relationship with her daughter.

Beyond the immediate parent-child dynamic, the practice of self-reflection and journaling can profoundly impact other areas of life. Improved self-awareness translates into stronger relationships with partners, friends, and colleagues. It enhances emotional regulation, leading to better stress management and improved mental health overall. By understanding our own emotional patterns and triggers, we become more equipped to handle challenging situations with greater composure and empathy. We become more adept at setting healthy boundaries, asserting our needs, and communicating effectively. This newfound self-assuredness extends to all facets of life, promoting personal growth and a greater sense of well-being.

There are numerous ways to incorporate journaling and self-reflection into daily life. It could be as simple as dedicating 15 minutes each morning or evening to writing down thoughts and feelings. Guided journaling prompts, readily available online or in self-help books, can provide a starting point for those who are unsure where to begin. Some find it

helpful to use specific prompts focusing on particular areas of concern, like patterns of communication within the family, unresolved emotional conflicts, or memories that continue to resonate. Others may choose to keep a gratitude journal, focusing on positive experiences and fostering a sense of appreciation. The key is to find a method that feels comfortable and sustainable, allowing for consistent practice and deeper self-exploration.

It's important to remember that this is a journey, not a destination. There will be days when self-reflection reveals difficult truths, and journaling might feel emotionally challenging. This is to be expected. It's during these moments that self-compassion is paramount. Treat yourself with the same kindness and understanding you would offer a friend facing similar challenges. Acknowledge the pain, allow yourself to feel it, and remember that this process is about growth and healing, not perfection. It's a process of ongoing discovery, leading to a deeper understanding of ourselves, our families, and the legacy of intergenerational trauma. Through consistent effort and self-compassion, we can break the cycle and pave the way for healthier, more fulfilling lives for ourselves and future generations.

Remember that this process is not solely about identifying and analyzing past traumas. It is equally important to focus on cultivating present-day well-being and building a positive future for ourselves and our children, free from the shadow of unresolved pain. The journey of self-discovery is a continuous evolution, and the rewards of increased self- awareness, emotional regulation, and stronger family bonds are invaluable. By consistently engaging with these practices of self-reflection and journaling, you empower yourself to create a more harmonious and fulfilling life, both for yourself and for the generations to come.

Chapter 10

A Path to Personal Healing

Building upon the foundation of self-awareness cultivated through self-reflection and journaling, we now arrive at a crucial juncture on the path to healing: forgiveness.

Forgiveness, often misunderstood as condoning harmful actions, is actually a powerful act of self-liberation. It's not about minimizing the hurt caused; instead, it's about releasing the grip of resentment and bitterness that can poison our minds and relationships, perpetuating the cycle of intergenerational trauma. This process involves forgiving ourselves for perceived shortcomings, mistakes, or inherited patterns of behavior, as well as forgiving others—parents, siblings, extended family members—who may have inflicted pain, consciously or unconsciously.

Forgiveness begins with acknowledging the pain. Suppressing or ignoring past hurts only allows them to fester, influencing our present-day interactions and creating barriers to genuine connection. It requires honestly confronting the emotions associated with the trauma, allowing ourselves to feel the anger, sadness, fear, or betrayal without judgment. This initial step can be incredibly challenging, particularly if we've grown accustomed to burying our emotions. It may involve intense emotional up-

61

heaval, and it's crucial to approach this process with self- compassion and seek support from a therapist or trusted friend if needed. Remember, there's no timetable for processing these emotions; allow yourself the time and space necessary to fully acknowledge and process the pain.

Once we've acknowledged the hurt, the next step involves understanding the context of the actions that caused it. This doesn't mean excusing abusive behavior, but rather seeking

to understand the underlying factors that may have contributed to it. This can involve exploring the experiences of our parents and ancestors, recognizing that their actions might have stemmed from their own unresolved trauma, pain, or lack of healthy coping mechanisms. It's a difficult truth to accept that some individuals may not be capable of taking responsibility for their actions, or might lack the emotional maturity to offer an apology or demonstrate remorse. Yet understanding their background can lessen the burden of carrying the weight of their actions alone. This perspective shift is critical in freeing ourselves from the chains of resentment. This isn't about excusing their behavior; it's about understanding the context that shaped it, which allows us to separate their actions from our self- worth.

Self-forgiveness is a particularly crucial aspect of this process. We often carry a heavy burden of self-blame, especially when dealing with intergenerational trauma. We may internalize the criticisms and judgments of our parents or ancestors, believing that we are somehow flawed or deficient. This self-criticism can hinder our ability to move forward, perpetuating a cycle of negative self-talk and self- sabotage. Self-forgiveness involves acknowledging our imperfections, accepting our past mistakes, and releasing the self-judgment that keeps us trapped. It's about recognizing that we are all works in progress, and that making mistakes is a natural part of the human experience. It's about extending to ourselves the same compassion and understanding we would offer a dear friend facing similar challenges.

The act of forgiving others is not a passive process; it demands active participation and a conscious decision. It is about shifting our perspective from a place of anger and resentment to a place of compassion and understanding. It

does not require reconciliation or even contact with the person we are forgiving. Forgiveness is primarily an internal process, a release of the negative emotions that bind us to the past. This might involve writing letters (un-sent if necessary) articulating our feelings and releasing our anger on paper, engaging in mindfulness practices to cultivate compassion, or utilizing therapeutic techniques, such as EMDR, to process traumatic memories.

The journey towards forgiveness is not linear. There will be setbacks, moments of doubt, and times when the pain resurfaces. It's essential to maintain self-compassion during these times and remember that forgiveness is a process, not a destination. It's okay to take breaks, to revisit earlier steps, and to allow yourself to feel the full range of emotions that arise. Celebrate small victories along the way, acknowledging the progress you've made and the strength you've shown.

Consider the example of Sarah, a woman struggling with an estranged relationship with her mother. Her mother had been emotionally distant and critical throughout Sarah's childhood, creating a deep-seated sense of insecurity and inadequacy. Through therapy, Sarah began to understand that her mother's behavior likely stemmed from her own unresolved trauma – her own difficult childhood and experiences of neglect. This understanding didn't erase the pain Sarah felt, but it shifted her perspective. It allowed her to start separating her mother's actions from her own inherent worth, recognizing that her mother's behavior was a reflection of her mother's struggles, not a reflection of Sarah's value. Sarah's journey to forgiveness wasn't about condoning her mother's behavior; it was about releasing the bitterness and resentment that had been weighing her down for years, allowing her to heal and build healthier relationships in her own life.

Another example is David, a man who struggled with intense feelings of guilt and self-blame for his family's financial difficulties. His father, facing job loss and mounting debt, had become increasingly volatile and emotionally distant.

David, as the eldest son, internalized the pressure and blame, believing he should have been able to prevent their hardship. Through journaling and self-reflection, David began to understand that he was a child at the time and could not have shouldered the financial burdens of his family. He realized his father's actions stemmed from a place of stress and desperation, not malice. By forgiving himself for the unrealistic expectations he placed on his younger self, David was able to release the self-blame and focus on building a more supportive relationship with his father. This wasn't a simple task; it required many sessions of therapy and self- reflection. However, the release of the burden of self-blame allowed him to process the events with greater clarity.

Forgiveness also plays a crucial role in repairing damaged relationships. While forgiveness doesn't necessitate reconciliation, it paves the way for healthier interactions, allowing us to let go of the resentment that fuels conflict and prevents genuine connection. Once we've forgiven ourselves and others, we can approach our relationships with more empathy, compassion, and understanding. We can establish healthier boundaries, express our needs more effectively, and communicate more constructively.

The benefits of forgiveness extend beyond our immediate relationships. It promotes emotional well-being, reducing stress, anxiety, and depression. Forgiveness allows us to break free from the cycle of negativity and focus on building a positive future. It empowers us to move forward, creating space for healthier relationships and a more fulfilling life.

This is not to diminish the seriousness of trauma or to

suggest that simply forgiving will erase the pain. The pain will still be there, a part of the narrative of our lives, but the choice to forgive allows us to process that pain constructively and choose to no longer carry its weight. It allows us to reclaim our power and shape our future.

However, the journey to forgiveness is not always simple and can sometimes feel overwhelming, particularly in the case of severe trauma or severe abuse. It is crucial to remember that seeking professional help from a therapist is not a sign of weakness, but a testament to your commitment to your healing. A therapist can provide guidance, support, and coping strategies to navigate this challenging process.

They can help you to unpack complex emotions, identify unhealthy patterns of thinking, and develop healthier coping mechanisms to manage the emotional toll of the journey. It is a testament to your strength and commitment to healing. The support and guidance of a qualified therapist can make a significant difference in the journey towards personal healing and building healthier relationships. Remember, healing is a process, not a destination, and you are not alone in this journey. The path to forgiveness is paved with understanding, compassion, and self-care, ultimately leading to a more fulfilling and peaceful life.

Chapter 11

Active Listening and Empathetic Responses

Active listening and empathetic responses are cornerstones of healthy parent-child communication. They form the bedrock upon which trust, understanding, and a secure attachment are built. In families grappling with the legacy of trauma, these skills become even more crucial, acting as a powerful antidote to the patterns of miscommunication and emotional disconnection often passed down through generations. Without active listening and empathy, misunderstandings easily escalate into conflict, reinforcing negative patterns and hindering the healing process. The absence of these skills can inadvertently perpetuate the cycle of trauma, leaving children feeling unheard, unseen, and unsupported.

Active listening is far more than simply hearing the words your child is saying. It involves fully engaging with their message – both verbal and nonverbal – demonstrating genuine interest and a commitment to understanding their perspective. This means setting aside your own thoughts and judgments, even if only temporarily, and focusing entirely on what your child is communicating. It's about creating a safe space where they feel comfortable expressing themselves without fear of interruption, criticism, or judgment. This space is vital for children, especially those who may have experienced trauma or grown up in an environment where their feelings were dismissed or invalidated.

Concretely, active listening involves several key techniques. First, maintain consistent eye contact, demonstrating that you are fully present and engaged with your child. Avoid distractions such as your phone or other tasks; give your child your undivided attention. Second, utilize nonverbal

cues to show that you are listening. Nodding your head, offering small affirmative sounds like "uh-huh" or "mm- hmm," and mirroring their body language (in a subtle, non- intrusive way) can all communicate your attentiveness and understanding.

Third, reflect back what you're hearing. This doesn't mean simply parroting your child's words. Rather, it involves summarizing their message in your own words, ensuring you accurately grasp their emotions and concerns. For example, if your child says, "I'm so mad! Nobody ever listens to me," you might respond with something like, "It sounds like you're feeling really frustrated and unheard right now. Can you tell me more about what happened?" This technique ensures clarity, validates your child's feelings, and opens the door for further dialogue.

Finally, ask clarifying questions to ensure you have a complete understanding of their perspective. Avoid interrupting or jumping to conclusions. Instead, patiently allow your child to fully express themselves. Even if their perspective differs from yours, acknowledge their feelings and validate their experience. Remember, the goal is not to necessarily "fix" the problem but to create a space of understanding and empathy. This approach helps children feel heard, seen, and respected, fostering a sense of safety and trust that is vital for healing from trauma and building a stronger parent-child relationship.

Empathy, the ability to understand and share the feelings of another, is equally vital. Empathy involves stepping into your child's shoes, trying to understand their perspective from their frame of reference. This requires setting aside your own biases and judgments and focusing on their emotional experience. This doesn't mean you necessarily agree with their actions or perspective, but it does mean

acknowledging and validating their feelings. When a child feels understood and accepted for who they are, even with their flaws and imperfections, it builds resilience and strengthens their sense of self-worth. This is particularly important for children who have experienced trauma, as they may have developed a low sense of self-worth or believe their feelings are invalid.

Demonstrating empathy involves more than simply saying, "I understand." Instead, it involves actively trying to understand the underlying emotions behind their words and behaviors. Often, a child's behavior – tantrums, defiance, or withdrawal – is a manifestation of unmet needs or underlying emotional pain. For instance, a child who consistently misbehaves at school might not just be acting out but could be feeling overwhelmed, anxious, or lonely. By seeking to understand the root cause of their behavior, you can offer more effective support and guidance.

In the context of intergenerational trauma, empathy is paramount. It allows you to recognize and address the ways in which past trauma may be impacting your parenting. For instance, if you grew up in a family where emotional expression was suppressed, you might inadvertently stifle your child's emotional expression. Becoming aware of these patterns is crucial to breaking the cycle of trauma. Empathy helps you recognize that your child's reactions, even if challenging, are often rooted in their experiences and that your response should be driven by compassion and understanding, not judgment or anger.

Here's a practical example: Imagine your teenager comes home upset after a fight with a friend. Instead of immediately launching into advice or criticism, try responding with empathy. You might say, "Honey, it sounds like you're really hurting right now. Can you tell me what

happened?" Then, actively listen, reflecting back what you hear and asking clarifying questions. You might say, "So it sounds like you feel betrayed by your friend, and that's really painful. It's okay to feel angry and hurt." This response validates your child's emotions, creating a safe space for them to process their feelings without fear of judgment.

Another scenario: Your young child is throwing a tantrum because they can't have another cookie. Instead of reprimanding them, try to understand their perspective. They may not have the language skills to articulate their feelings, but their behavior is communicating something. Try squatting down to their level, making eye contact, and saying, "It seems like you really want another cookie, and you're feeling very frustrated that you can't have one right now. That's understandable." Even if you don't give them another cookie, acknowledging their feelings demonstrates empathy and reduces the likelihood of further escalation.

These examples highlight how active listening and empathetic responses are interconnected. Active listening creates a foundation for understanding your child's perspective, while empathy allows you to connect with their emotions on a deeper level. Together, these skills form a powerful tool for building stronger, healthier parent-child relationships, breaking cycles of trauma, and fostering a more nurturing family environment. Consistent practice of these techniques can profoundly transform your interactions with your children, creating a space for genuine connection, understanding, and healing. Remember, the goal is not perfection but progress. Each effort to practice active listening and empathy is a step towards creating a more compassionate and supportive family dynamic, and ultimately, a brighter future for your children. This approach, while demanding patience and self-reflection, offers the

promise of building more resilient, emotionally intelligent children and fostering stronger, healthier parent-child bonds.

Chapter 12

Effective Communication Strategies

Building upon the foundation of active listening and empathy, effective communication extends to mastering clear and assertive expression. This doesn't mean aggressive confrontation, but rather a skillful way to express your needs and boundaries without causing defensiveness or escalating conflict. It's about conveying your message with respect while ensuring your voice is heard. This involves choosing the right time and place, selecting appropriate words, and using nonverbal cues to reinforce your message. When children feel heard and understood, even when there's a disagreement, it fosters a sense of safety and trust, crucial for navigating the complex dynamics of a family grappling with intergenerational trauma. The absence of clear communication can lead to misunderstandings, resentment, and ultimately, a breakdown in the parent-child relationship.

One crucial aspect of assertive communication is the use of "I" statements. Instead of blaming ("You always leave your clothes on the floor!"), focus on expressing your feelings and needs ("I feel frustrated when I see clothes on the floor because it makes it difficult to keep the house clean"). This shifts the focus from accusation to personal experience, making it less likely to trigger a defensive response.

Children are more receptive to understanding their impact when presented with factual observations rather than accusatory pronouncements. This approach encourages them to take responsibility for their actions without feeling attacked.

Furthermore, nonverbal communication plays a significant role. Maintaining eye contact (without staring intensely), using an open and approachable posture, and mirroring your

child's body language (to a reasonable extent) can convey empathy and understanding. Conversely, crossed arms, averted gaze, or a dismissive tone can inadvertently shut down communication. Paying attention to nonverbal cues from your child is equally important. Their body language might reveal emotions they are struggling to articulate verbally. A slumped posture, fidgeting, or avoidance of eye contact could indicate anxiety, discomfort, or reluctance to engage. Learning to recognize these nonverbal cues allows for a more nuanced understanding of your child's experience and facilitates a more responsive and empathetic interaction.

Effective communication also requires careful timing and setting. Avoid addressing sensitive issues when you're stressed, rushed, or emotionally overwhelmed. Choose a time when both you and your child are calm and receptive. The setting should be private and conducive to open dialogue, free from distractions. A quiet space, free from interruptions, fosters a more relaxed atmosphere and enables a deeper, more meaningful conversation. This environment reduces the likelihood of misunderstandings or misinterpretations, which can easily escalate in stressful or rushed situations. Choosing the right time also respects your child's emotional state. A child already struggling with anxieties or overwhelmed by emotions is far less likely to engage constructively in a conversation.

Another essential skill is active listening, which we touched upon earlier, but its importance warrants further emphasis in the context of assertive communication. Active listening isn't just about hearing your child's words; it's about understanding their perspective, their emotions, and the underlying message. This requires actively paying attention, reflecting back what you hear ("So, it sounds like you're feeling frustrated because..."), and asking clarifying questions to ensure complete understanding. When children

feel truly heard, they are more likely to be receptive to your perspective. This reciprocity fosters a sense of mutual respect and encourages open dialogue.

Furthermore, learning to identify and address your own emotional responses is critical for effective communication. When faced with challenging behavior or difficult conversations, it's essential to manage your own emotions first. Take a moment to breathe, center yourself, and regulate your emotional state before engaging in conversation. This prevents emotional reactivity, which can disrupt communication and escalate conflict. Techniques like deep breathing, mindfulness, or taking a brief break can be helpful in managing your emotions and preventing impulsive reactions. This self-regulation ensures you can respond with empathy and understanding, rather than reacting defensively or becoming overwhelmed by your own feelings.

Managing conflict constructively is another vital component of effective communication. Disagreements are inevitable in any family, but the way you handle them significantly impacts the overall dynamics. Avoid resorting to shouting, insults, or personal attacks. Instead, focus on the issue at hand, using "I" statements to express your feelings and needs. Encourage your child to do the same, creating a space where both of you feel heard and respected, even amidst disagreement. This approach, however, requires a degree of self-awareness and patience. It requires you to acknowledge your own emotional responses and reactions and take steps to manage them constructively before engaging in conflict resolution.

Setting clear and consistent boundaries is also crucial. Boundaries protect both you and your child, providing a sense of safety and structure. Clearly defined boundaries help children understand expectations and limits, reducing

confusion and potential conflict. For example, setting clear rules about screen time or bedtime routines can minimize power struggles and promote a more orderly and predictable environment. This consistency builds predictability and stability for the child, significantly reducing anxiety. The predictability offered by boundaries helps children feel safe and secure, especially those navigating the effects of intergenerational trauma. The more consistent the boundaries, the more secure a child feels.

Negotiation and compromise play an important role in conflict resolution and boundary setting. While boundaries are essential, inflexibility can lead to resentment and power struggles. Involve your child in the process of setting boundaries whenever possible, allowing them to express their input and participate in finding mutually acceptable solutions. This participatory approach fosters a sense of ownership and responsibility, strengthening the parent-child bond. Negotiation also teaches valuable life skills to children, such as compromise, empathy, and problem- solving. Children learn to consider other perspectives and find solutions that satisfy everyone's needs.

Finally, regular family meetings can provide a dedicated space for open communication. These meetings, conducted in a supportive and non-judgmental atmosphere, offer a structured opportunity to discuss concerns, address issues, and strengthen family bonds. They can also provide a platform for expressing appreciation and celebrating accomplishments, fostering a sense of positivity and connection. This regular scheduled time for open communication helps prevent minor issues from escalating into significant conflicts. It allows for the identification and discussion of problems before they become overwhelming. The regular dialogue fosters trust and opens a continuous

channel of communication that helps families weather storms and build strong, resilient bonds.

In conclusion, effective communication is not merely about exchanging words; it's about building trust, understanding, and fostering a secure connection. By actively listening, expressing yourself clearly and assertively, managing conflict constructively, setting healthy boundaries, and creating opportunities for regular dialogue, you can create a nurturing environment that promotes healing and strengthens the parent-child relationship. This intentional approach to communication can break cycles of intergenerational trauma and pave the way for healthier family dynamics, fostering resilience and emotional well-being for generations to come. Remember, the journey toward healthier communication is a process, not a destination. Be patient with yourself and your child, celebrating small victories and learning from setbacks. The investment in improving communication will yield significant rewards in strengthening your relationship and

Chapter 13

NonViolent Communication in Practice

promoting the well-being of your entire family.

Building on the foundation of effective communication established in the previous chapter, we now delve into the practical application of Non-Violent Communication (NVC) within the parent-child dynamic. NVC, developed by Marshall Rosenberg, offers a powerful framework for navigating conflict and fostering empathy, particularly crucial when dealing with the complexities of intergenerational trauma. It emphasizes expressing needs honestly and respectfully, while simultaneously understanding and validating the needs of others. This approach shifts the focus from blame and judgment to understanding underlying emotions and motivations, a significant step toward healing fractured relationships.

The core of NVC rests on four key components: observations, feelings, needs, and requests. Let's examine each in the context of parent-child interactions, using real- life scenarios to illustrate their application.

Observations: This step requires separating objective facts from subjective interpretations. Instead of saying, "You're always messy," which is a judgment, an observation would be, "I see clothes on the floor in your bedroom." The difference is subtle but crucial. Judgments trigger defensiveness; observations invite dialogue. Consider a child consistently interrupting conversations. An observational statement would be, "I noticed you interrupted me three times during our conversation." This avoids accusatory language like "You're so rude," which shuts down communication.

Feelings: Once an observation is made, identify the accompanying feelings. Instead of saying "You make me angry," which is assigning responsibility, express your own feelings: "I feel frustrated when I repeatedly have to clean up your room." Children need to understand that your emotions are your responsibility, not theirs. This allows them to engage with your emotional state without feeling blamed.

For the interrupting child, you might say, "I feel a little unheard when I'm interrupted repeatedly." This honest expression of your feelings lays the groundwork for empathetic understanding.

Needs: This is the heart of NVC. Identify the underlying needs that are driving your feelings. Behind frustration about a messy room might be the need for order, respect, or cooperation. Behind feeling unheard might be the need for connection, attention, or validation. Articulating these needs clarifies your motivations, moving beyond surface-level emotions. For the messy room, you might explain: "I need a clean and organized space so I feel calm and relaxed at home." For the interruptions, you could say: "I need to feel heard and respected during conversations so we can connect better." This transparently communicates your needs, encouraging empathy and understanding in your child.

Requests: This step involves making concrete, actionable requests, rather than demands. Instead of "Clean your room now!", a request could be: "Could you please help me clean your room by putting away your clothes? We can work together." For the interrupting child, a request could be: "When I'm speaking, could you please wait your turn to talk? I want to make sure we both feel heard." Clearly stated requests that are specific and achievable are more likely to be met than vague commands or demands.

Let's illustrate these four steps with a practical example. Imagine a scenario where a teenager consistently stays up late, missing school and impacting their well-being:

Observation: "I noticed you haven't been attending morning classes recently."

Feeling: "I feel worried and concerned about your well- being and academic success."

Need: "My needs are for you to thrive, to be healthy and to be successful. This includes being rested enough for school and attending classes."

Request: "Would you be willing to work with me to establish a consistent bedtime routine? Perhaps we can explore adjusting your schedule together to find a balance between rest and recreation?"

Another example might be a child who refuses to eat their vegetables:

Observation: "I see that you've left all your vegetables on your plate."

Feeling: "I feel a little disappointed because I made sure the meal was healthy and nutritious."

Need: "My need is for you to be healthy and strong, and eating your vegetables is part of that."

Request: "Would you be open to trying one bite of broccoli, and if you don't like it, we can discuss alternative vegetables you might prefer?"

It's important to remember that NVC isn't a magic bullet. It requires practice, patience, and a willingness to understand your child's perspective. Children who have experienced trauma may require additional patience and understanding, as their behaviors might stem from unresolved emotional pain. The goal isn't necessarily to change their behavior immediately, but to build a strong foundation of empathy and communication that allows for healing and growth.

Applying NVC might initially feel awkward or unnatural, particularly if you're accustomed to more authoritarian parenting styles. It is a shift in mindset and requires consistent practice. It's helpful to start with smaller interactions and gradually incorporate it into more challenging situations. Begin by practicing self-compassion, acknowledging that learning NVC takes time and effort. It is a journey, not a destination, and small steps towards improved communication will reap rewards over time.

The impact of intergenerational trauma can manifest in various ways, influencing communication styles within families. For instance, a parent who experienced emotional neglect as a child might struggle to express affection or validate their child's feelings. Similarly, a parent who experienced frequent conflict in their childhood might inadvertently recreate similar patterns in their own family. Understanding these patterns is crucial for applying NVC effectively.

In families grappling with intergenerational trauma, emotions can run high, making constructive communication even more challenging. However, NVC provides a framework for navigating these challenges. By focusing on observing without judgment, expressing feelings without blame, identifying underlying needs, and making specific requests, parents can create a more empathetic and understanding environment. This environment fosters emotional safety and reduces the risk of perpetuating unhealthy communication patterns.

A crucial element of NVC is active listening. This goes beyond simply hearing words; it involves paying attention to non-verbal cues, reflecting back what the child is saying to ensure understanding, and validating their feelings, even if you don't agree with their perspective. When children feel truly heard and understood, they are more likely to open up and engage in constructive dialogue. This active listening is particularly essential when dealing with the complexities of intergenerational trauma, as it creates space for children to express their emotions safely and without fear of judgment.

It is also important to practice self-care while applying NVC. Parenting is demanding, and the additional burden of addressing intergenerational trauma can be emotionally taxing. Parents who prioritize self-care, seeking support when needed, are better equipped to handle challenges and maintain a compassionate approach to communication. This might involve seeking therapy, joining support groups, or engaging in stress-reducing activities. Self-care isn't selfish; it's a necessary component of effective parenting and healthy family relationships.

By consistently applying the principles of NVC, parents can create a more harmonious and nurturing family environment, fostering resilience and emotional well-being for both themselves and their children. The process is iterative; it requires ongoing learning and adjustment. Celebrate small victories, learn from setbacks, and remember that the investment in improved communication yields significant rewards in strengthening family bonds and promoting healing across generations. The journey towards healthier communication is a testament to your commitment to breaking cycles of trauma and building a stronger, more loving family. This investment in mindful communication is an investment in the future well-being of your family, contributing to a legacy of healing and healthy relationships. The transformation begins with the willingness to listen deeply, to express needs clearly, and to foster a culture of empathy within your family. Remember that the ultimate goal is not just effective communication, but the creation of a loving and supportive environment where each family member feels seen, heard, and understood. This is where true healing begins.

Chapter 14

Setting Healthy Boundaries with Children

Building upon the foundation of empathetic communication established in the previous chapter, we now turn our attention to a crucial element of healthy parenting: setting boundaries. Boundaries, often misunderstood as restrictive or punitive, are in fact essential for fostering a child's healthy development and reducing conflict within the family. They provide a sense of security and predictability, crucial elements for children grappling with the complexities of intergenerational trauma. Children who grow up without clear boundaries often struggle with self-regulation, emotional instability, and difficulty in forming healthy relationships later in life. Conversely, well-defined boundaries empower children, teaching them self-respect and respect for others. This is particularly crucial for children exposed to family patterns of emotional neglect, abuse, or chaotic relationships, as clear boundaries offer a stabilizing force amidst uncertainty. It's about creating a framework that allows for both freedom and responsibility.

Setting boundaries effectively isn't about control; it's about creating a safe and predictable environment. It's about teaching children the limits of acceptable behavior, and providing them with a sense of structure that allows them to flourish. For example, establishing consistent bedtimes, mealtimes, and screen-time limits provides a sense of order and predictability. This is particularly helpful for children who've experienced inconsistent parenting or trauma. The predictability reduces anxiety and helps them develop healthy routines. Furthermore, these boundaries are not arbitrary; they are rooted in the child's developmental needs and the family's overall well-being.

It's important to remember that setting boundaries isn't a one-time event. It's an ongoing process that requires consistent reinforcement and adaptation as the child grows and matures. The boundaries you set with a toddler will differ from those you set with a teenager. The key is to maintain consistency and communicate clearly. Children thrive on consistency. Knowing what to expect reduces anxiety and promotes feelings of safety and security.

Inconsistency, on the other hand, can lead to confusion, insecurity, and acting out. Therefore, parents need to work together to ensure that boundaries are consistently enforced, even when it's difficult.

Consider, for instance, a family grappling with the legacy of substance abuse. Establishing clear boundaries around alcohol and drug use is vital, not only for the child's safety but also for modeling healthy behavior. This might involve creating a drug-free home environment, openly discussing the dangers of substance abuse, and seeking professional help if needed. Setting boundaries in this context is not about punishment; it's about protection and modeling healthy coping mechanisms. This is about teaching children that their feelings matter and are valid, and that they deserve to feel safe and protected.

Another common area where boundaries are essential is around physical and emotional safety. Children who have experienced trauma often have difficulty distinguishing between healthy and unhealthy touch, and setting healthy boundaries around physical affection is therefore paramount. This requires open and age-appropriate communication about personal space, consent, and the importance of reporting any inappropriate physical contact. Similarly, setting boundaries around emotional abuse is crucial. This includes teaching children that it is not okay for anyone to verbally abuse or belittle them, and empowering them to

assert their right to feel respected and valued. Setting these boundaries may involve implementing clear consequences for violating these rules, and actively teaching children how to express their needs and feelings in a healthy and assertive manner.

For instance, a child exposed to parental conflict characterized by yelling or verbal abuse might benefit from explicitly defining respectful communication within the family. This could include rules against yelling or name- calling, replacing aggressive communication with calm and respectful dialogue. Children need to learn that their feelings are valid, and that they deserve to be treated with respect, regardless of the challenges within the family system. The goal is to create a space where emotional safety is prioritized, thus providing an antidote to the emotional instability they may have experienced.

Setting boundaries also extends to personal time and space. Respecting a child's need for solitude and personal space is crucial for their healthy development. This involves allowing them to have their own private space, respecting their privacy, and not intruding on their personal activities unless necessary. This is especially critical for children who have experienced neglect or invasion of their personal boundaries. This may mean having a private space in the house, whether it's their bedroom or a designated corner, where they can feel safe and alone.

However, it's critical to understand that setting boundaries effectively is not about imposing rigid rules. It's about finding a balance between structure and flexibility. This requires understanding the child's developmental stage and individual needs. A young child requires more structure and guidance than a teenager, and the methods for setting boundaries will need to adapt accordingly. Consistent and

clear communication is crucial; children need to understand why boundaries are being set and how these boundaries contribute to their safety and well-being. It's not enough to simply dictate rules; explaining the reasoning behind them is vital for fostering cooperation and understanding.

Furthermore, setting boundaries extends beyond the parent-child relationship and encompasses the broader family system. If a family member is consistently engaging in disruptive or harmful behavior, setting clear boundaries with that individual is crucial. This may involve limiting contact, establishing clear communication protocols, or seeking professional help if needed. These boundaries protect the child from harm and model healthy relationships.

The process of setting boundaries may involve conflict. Children will inevitably test boundaries. This is a natural part of development, and should not be viewed as defiance, but as an opportunity for teaching and reinforcing healthy limits. Consistency in enforcing consequences is crucial.

Children need to understand that actions have consequences, and these consequences should be consistently applied to ensure predictability and fairness. It's about teaching self- regulation and responsibility, rather than simply punishing misbehavior.

When dealing with a child who is resisting boundaries, it's crucial to approach the situation with empathy and understanding. Instead of reacting with anger or frustration, try to understand the underlying reasons for the resistance. Is the child feeling insecure, overwhelmed, or unheard? By addressing the underlying emotional needs, you can often address the behavior. Active listening and validation are vital in this process. Let the child know that their feelings are important, even if their behavior isn't acceptable. This

process fosters trust and strengthens the parent-child relationship.

It's also essential for parents to reflect on their own boundaries and needs. Parents who are struggling with their own unresolved trauma may have difficulty setting boundaries. It's crucial to seek professional help to address these personal challenges, as unresolved trauma can significantly impact parenting styles and the ability to create healthy boundaries for children. Self-care is an essential component of effective boundary-setting. Parents need to prioritize their own physical and mental well-being to create a stable and supportive environment for their children.

Furthermore, remember that setting boundaries involves not only limiting unwanted behaviors, but also actively promoting positive ones. By focusing on rewarding positive behaviors rather than solely punishing negative ones, parents can create a more positive and supportive environment, fostering cooperation and a sense of accomplishment in children.

Finally, it's important to remember that setting healthy boundaries is a journey, not a destination. It requires ongoing effort, patience, and self-reflection. There will be setbacks and challenges, but consistent effort will eventually lead to a healthier and more harmonious family dynamic. The investment in establishing healthy boundaries is an investment in the future well-being of the child and the entire family, contributing to a legacy of healthier relationships across generations. The goal is to create a loving and supportive environment where every family member feels seen, heard, understood and empowered to establish their own healthy boundaries, thus breaking the cycles of trauma and building a stronger, more resilient family.

Chapter 15

Creating a Safe and Supportive Environment

Creating a safe and supportive environment is the cornerstone of healthy parent-child communication and breaking the cycle of intergenerational trauma. It's more than just the absence of conflict; it's the active cultivation of a space where children feel seen, heard, understood, and unconditionally loved. This involves a multifaceted approach that addresses both the physical and emotional needs of the child, acknowledging the profound impact of past experiences on present-day dynamics.

The physical environment plays a surprisingly significant role. A home characterized by chaos, unpredictability, or even subtle cues of tension can be incredibly destabilizing for a child, especially one grappling with the legacy of trauma. Consider the visual aspects: is the home cluttered and overwhelming, or is it organized and calming? Is there a designated space where the child can retreat for quiet time and reflection? A child's bedroom, for instance, should be a sanctuary – a place of comfort and security where they can feel safe to be themselves. This might involve creating a calming corner with soft blankets, favorite books, or calming sensory items like a lava lamp or a soft textured blanket. The color palette, lighting, and even the scent of the room can contribute to the overall feeling of safety and tranquility.

Beyond the physical, the emotional climate is paramount. This requires a conscious effort to create a culture of empathy, respect, and open communication. One crucial aspect is predictability. Children thrive on routines and knowing what to expect. Consistent bedtimes, mealtimes, and family activities provide a sense of security and stability, particularly crucial for children exposed to inconsistent or

chaotic family patterns in the past. Establish clear expectations and rules, but ensure that these rules are explained clearly and consistently enforced, avoiding arbitrary punishment or inconsistent discipline. Children need to understand the reasons behind the rules, fostering a sense of fairness and collaboration rather than fear or coercion.

Active listening is another vital component. This involves truly hearing what your child is saying, both verbally and nonverbally. It's not just about listening to respond, but listening to understand. Put aside distractions, make eye contact, and reflect back what you've heard to ensure accurate understanding. This shows your child that their thoughts and feelings are valued and respected. Often, children struggling with the impact of intergenerational trauma may not express themselves directly. They might exhibit behavioral issues, emotional outbursts, or withdrawal. Paying close attention to these nonverbal cues is crucial for identifying underlying emotional distress. For example, a child's sudden clinginess or aggressive behavior might be a manifestation of underlying anxiety or fear related to past experiences. Active listening enables you to address these underlying concerns rather than simply reacting to the surface behavior.

Validating your child's emotions, even negative ones, is crucial. This doesn't mean agreeing with their behavior; it means acknowledging their feelings as legitimate and understandable. Phrases like, "I understand you're feeling angry right now," or, "It sounds like you're feeling really hurt," can make a significant difference. This helps children develop emotional literacy and self-awareness, empowering them to process their emotions in a healthy way. Avoid dismissing or minimizing their feelings, as this can reinforce feelings of invalidation and isolation. Remember, the goal is

not to fix their feelings but to help them feel heard and understood.

Empathy is essential in understanding the impact of intergenerational trauma. It requires placing yourself in your child's shoes and trying to understand their experiences from their perspective. This means recognizing that their behaviors might stem from past experiences they may not even fully understand. It might be helpful to consider your own childhood experiences and how they might have shaped your parenting style. Acknowledging the impact of intergenerational trauma allows for greater compassion and understanding in your interactions. A child who has witnessed domestic violence, for instance, might react fearfully to even minor disagreements, reflecting the lingering trauma of their past. Recognizing this can lead to a more patient and understanding approach.

Setting clear and consistent boundaries, as discussed in the previous chapter, is equally critical. Boundaries protect both the parent and the child, creating a sense of security and predictability. However, these boundaries must be set with empathy and understanding, taking into account the child's developmental stage and unique needs. For example, a young child might require more structured boundaries than an adolescent, and a child experiencing significant trauma might need a more gradual and supportive approach. It's important to communicate boundaries clearly and consistently, avoiding ambiguity or inconsistency.

Inconsistency undermines trust and can lead to increased anxiety and insecurity in the child.

Forgiveness is another critical aspect of creating a safe and supportive environment, both for the child and for yourself. Forgiveness does not mean condoning past behaviors or erasing the pain caused by trauma. It's about releasing the

resentment and anger that can hinder healing and growth. Forgiveness allows you to move forward and focus on building a healthier relationship with your child, free from the weight of past hurts. This process might involve seeking professional guidance, engaging in self-reflection, and actively working on releasing past grievances. It's a personal journey that takes time and patience but is essential for breaking the cycle of intergenerational trauma.

Building a safe and supportive environment is an ongoing process, not a destination. It requires consistent effort, self-awareness, and a willingness to learn and adapt. It's about creating a space where your child feels unconditionally loved, accepted, and empowered to be their authentic self. This involves creating a physically and emotionally safe space, practicing active listening, validating emotions, setting clear boundaries, and fostering empathy and forgiveness. By prioritizing these elements, parents can create a nurturing environment that fosters healthy development, strengthens parent-child bonds, and ultimately breaks the cycle of intergenerational trauma, paving the way for healthier relationships and greater well-being for future generations. Remember, the investment in creating this safe space is an investment in your child's future and the well-being of your family as a whole.

It's also vital to recognize that seeking professional support is a sign of strength, not weakness. A therapist specializing in trauma and intergenerational relationships can provide invaluable guidance and support in navigating the complexities of healing past wounds and fostering healthier family dynamics. Therapy provides a safe and confidential space to explore unresolved issues, develop coping mechanisms, and learn strategies for effective communication and boundary setting. They can help you understand the impact of your own family history on your

parenting style and equip you with the tools to break free from unhealthy patterns. This professional guidance can significantly enhance your ability to create a truly safe and supportive environment for your child and foster a legacy of healthier family relationships.

Furthermore, consider engaging in self-care practices. Parenting, particularly when grappling with intergenerational trauma, can be emotionally demanding. Prioritizing your own well-being is crucial to your ability to provide a safe and supportive environment for your child. Engage in activities that bring you joy, relaxation, and rejuvenation.

This might include exercise, meditation, spending time in nature, pursuing hobbies, or connecting with supportive friends and family. Taking care of yourself isn't selfish; it's essential for your emotional resilience and your ability to effectively parent. Remember that you are not alone in this journey; seeking support from others, whether it be family, friends, or professionals, is a sign of strength. By nurturing your own well-being, you're better equipped to create a loving, secure, and supportive environment for your child.

Finally, remember that this is a journey, not a destination. There will be setbacks and challenges along the way.

Moments of frustration, anger, or disconnection are inevitable. The key is to acknowledge these moments, learn from them, and continue striving toward your goal of creating a safe and supportive environment. Celebrate small victories along the way and remember that progress, not perfection, is the ultimate measure of success. By maintaining consistent effort, empathy, and a commitment to ongoing learning and growth, you can create a legacy of healthier family relationships that breaks the cycle of intergenerational trauma and fosters well-being for generations to come. The unwavering commitment to creating this space, filled with love, understanding, and

unwavering support, will contribute significantly to your child's emotional well-being and help foster a healthier, more resilient family dynamic.

Chapter 16

Conflict Resolution Skills for Parents

Conflict resolution is a crucial skill for any parent, but it takes on added significance when navigating the complexities of intergenerational trauma. Unresolved trauma can manifest in various ways within families, leading to heightened emotional reactivity, communication breakdowns, and frequent conflicts. For parents carrying the weight of past experiences, understanding and employing effective conflict resolution strategies is not merely beneficial; it's essential for building healthy parent-child relationships and breaking the cycle of trauma transmission. This doesn't mean conflicts will disappear entirely—healthy families experience disagreements—but the *way* you navigate these disagreements significantly impacts your children's emotional well-being and future relationships.

The first step in effective conflict resolution is shifting your mindset. Instead of viewing disagreements as battles to be won or lost, consider them opportunities for connection and growth. This perspective shift requires self-compassion and a willingness to understand your child's perspective, even when their behavior is challenging. Remember, a child's actions often stem from their emotional state, not necessarily a deliberate attempt to defy or upset you. Understanding the root cause of their behavior—which may be related to their own experiences or simply developmental stage—is crucial in addressing the conflict constructively.

Before diving into specific techniques, let's address the elephant in the room: your own emotional responses. Past trauma can trigger intense emotional reactions, making it difficult to respond calmly to conflict. If you find yourself feeling overwhelmed by anger, frustration, or anxiety during

a disagreement with your child, taking a pause is crucial. This isn't about ignoring the problem, but about managing your own emotional state before engaging in a discussion that could escalate. Remove yourself from the situation temporarily – go to another room, take a few deep breaths, engage in a calming activity like listening to music or taking a short walk – until you feel more composed. Then, return to the situation with a renewed sense of calm and clarity.

Once you've regulated your emotions, you can employ various conflict resolution techniques. Active listening is paramount. This involves truly hearing your child's perspective without interrupting or formulating your response while they're still speaking. Show genuine interest in what they're saying, even if you don't agree. Use verbal and nonverbal cues to demonstrate your attention – maintain eye contact, nod your head, and summarize their points to confirm your understanding. For example, instead of immediately jumping in with a solution, try saying, "So, it sounds like you're feeling frustrated because..." or "I hear you saying that... Can you tell me more about that?"

Empathy, the ability to understand and share the feelings of another, is another key element. This doesn't necessarily mean agreeing with your child's viewpoint, but it does mean validating their feelings. Acknowledging their emotions, even if you disagree with their actions, shows them you care about their emotional well-being. Phrases like "I understand why you're upset," or "That sounds really frustrating," can go a long way in de-escalating a tense situation.

Collaboratively finding solutions is a powerful method. Instead of imposing a solution, involve your child in the process. Ask for their input, brainstorm together, and consider various options. This approach fosters a sense of ownership and responsibility, making them more likely to

cooperate with the chosen solution. It also teaches valuable problem-solving skills that will benefit them throughout their lives. For example, if a conflict arises over screen time, instead of dictating the rules, you can discuss potential solutions together – perhaps creating a visual schedule or implementing a reward system.

Setting clear and consistent boundaries is essential, particularly when dealing with challenging behaviours. These boundaries should be age-appropriate and clearly communicated. Consistency is key; enforcing boundaries inconsistently can be more confusing and frustrating for children. When enforcing boundaries, it's crucial to remain calm and firm. Explain the reasons behind the boundary in age-appropriate language, and offer alternatives or compromises where possible. For instance, if your child is misbehaving, clearly state the consequence, such as losing a privilege, but also offer an opportunity to make amends or earn back the privilege.

Remember, conflict resolution is a skill that develops over time. It's a process of learning and adapting. Don't be discouraged if you don't master it overnight. Each conflict is a learning opportunity, both for you and your child.

Reflecting on the interactions after they have calmed down allows you to learn what worked well and what could be improved. Journaling can be a helpful tool for this reflective process. Note down successful strategies, areas for improvement, and recurring patterns in your communication style.

Consider seeking professional support if conflicts become frequent, intense, or consistently unresolved. A therapist specializing in family dynamics and trauma can provide guidance, tools, and strategies tailored to your specific family situation. They can help you identify underlying

issues contributing to the conflicts and develop personalized strategies for managing difficult emotions and improving communication. Family therapy can provide a safe and structured environment for open communication and collaborative problem-solving.

Beyond conflict resolution techniques, fostering a positive and supportive family environment is crucial in preventing conflict escalation. This involves creating a culture of respect, empathy, and open communication. Regular family meetings can provide a designated time for discussing issues, expressing concerns, and collaboratively making decisions.

These meetings can become a space for problem-solving as a unit, teaching children valuable skills in communication and cooperation. Remember to prioritize quality time together, engaging in activities that promote connection and strengthen family bonds. This shared time fosters a sense of belonging, security, and emotional closeness, reducing the likelihood of conflict. Creating a strong, secure attachment is one of the most effective buffers against conflict and promotes healthy emotional development.

Incorporating mindful practices into your daily routine can also significantly impact your ability to manage conflict effectively. Mindfulness involves paying attention to the present moment without judgment. This practice can help you regulate your emotions, respond more calmly to stressful situations, and foster self-awareness. Practicing mindfulness techniques, such as deep breathing exercises or meditation, can help you cultivate a sense of inner peace and calm, which are essential for navigating conflicts constructively.

These practices can be beneficial for both parents and children.

Finally, remember that your own self-care is inextricably linked to your ability to effectively resolve conflicts.

Prioritizing your mental and emotional health is not selfish; it's essential for your well-being and your ability to be a present and supportive parent. Engaging in activities that bring you joy and relaxation, such as spending time in nature, pursuing hobbies, or connecting with supportive friends, can help you replenish your emotional reserves and approach conflicts with a renewed sense of calm and resilience. Burnout is a significant factor in parental conflict; addressing it early on is crucial to sustaining a healthy family dynamic. Self-compassion, and understanding that you are doing the best you can with the resources you have, is critical in maintaining a healthy balance between parenting and self-care.

By implementing these strategies, you are not only addressing immediate conflicts but also actively contributing to the long-term emotional health of your children and fostering a more harmonious and resilient family environment. Remember that consistent effort and a commitment to personal growth are key to breaking the cycle of generational trauma and cultivating healthier family dynamics. The journey may not always be easy, but the rewards of creating a more loving and supportive family environment are immeasurable. The ability to navigate conflict constructively is a valuable life skill, and by teaching your children these skills, you are equipping them with the tools they need to thrive in their own relationships.

Chapter 17

Managing Tantrums and Challenging Behaviours

Understanding a child's tantrum or challenging behavior isn't simply about extinguishing the immediate outburst; it's about understanding the underlying needs and emotions driving the behavior. Often, these behaviors are not arbitrary acts of defiance, but rather expressions of unmet needs, anxieties stemming from past experiences, or a struggle to regulate emotions – all potentially rooted in intergenerational trauma. A child who consistently lashes out might be struggling with feelings of insecurity, abandonment, or overwhelming stress, mirroring patterns passed down through family generations. The key is to move beyond simply reacting to the behavior and instead understanding its root cause. This requires patience, empathy, and a willingness to explore the child's emotional landscape.

For instance, a child who throws a tantrum when their request is denied might not simply be seeking a specific object or privilege; they may be expressing a deeper feeling of lack of control, perhaps mirroring a family history where their voice was unheard or their needs consistently overlooked. Similarly, aggressive behavior could stem from learned patterns of conflict resolution observed within the family, where anger and aggression were utilized to express needs or assert control. Recognizing these patterns is crucial. We must analyze the family history, identifying potential triggers and reactions that mirror the child's behavior.

Effective management of these challenging behaviors begins with fostering a secure attachment between parent and child. This involves creating a safe space where the child feels comfortable expressing their emotions without fear of judgment or punishment. Active listening is key; truly

hearing what the child is communicating, both verbally and nonverbally, is crucial to understanding the underlying need. This might involve observing their body language, tone of voice, and facial expressions, understanding that these are often more revealing than words alone. A child's seemingly irrational anger might stem from a previous experience where they felt disregarded or misunderstood. The consistency of parental presence and reassurance during these moments greatly contributes to building a secure foundation, allowing the child to feel safe expressing their emotions.

When a tantrum or challenging behavior arises, the immediate goal is to regulate the child's emotional state. This does not mean suppressing the behavior, but rather guiding the child to find healthier coping mechanisms. Instead of reprimanding or punishing, try to validate their feelings.

Phrases like "I see you're really upset," or "It sounds like you're feeling frustrated," acknowledge the child's emotional experience, creating a sense of understanding and empathy. This validation, particularly crucial when dealing with trauma's effects, is a powerful tool in de-escalating the situation.

Once the child's emotional state is calmer, you can start to address the underlying need. This requires patient investigation and open communication. Ask open-ended questions like, "What happened that made you feel this way?" or "What do you need right now?" Avoid leading questions that might suggest a specific answer. The goal is to help the child articulate their needs and feelings, providing them with the language to express what's happening internally. This process often requires modeling healthy emotional expression, demonstrating how to communicate needs and feelings in a constructive way, especially important if generational patterns involved suppressing

emotions. This modelling is a vital part of breaking the cycle of unhealthy emotional responses.

Positive reinforcement is another effective tool. Instead of focusing solely on negative behaviors, actively praise and reward positive actions. When a child shows self-control, problem-solving skills, or attempts to communicate effectively, acknowledge their efforts with genuine appreciation. This reinforcement strengthens desired behaviors and creates a positive association with self- regulation. It helps the child develop a sense of self-efficacy and belief in their ability to manage their emotions.

Furthermore, teaching children effective coping mechanisms is crucial. These might include deep breathing exercises, mindfulness techniques, or simply finding a quiet space to calm down. These skills are essential for managing stress and emotional overload, particularly in children who have experienced trauma or are living in emotionally chaotic environments. Consistency in teaching and practicing these techniques builds resilience and empowers the child to take control of their emotional responses.

Incorporating elements of play therapy can be immensely beneficial, particularly when dealing with trauma. Play offers a non-threatening medium for children to express their emotions, work through anxieties, and process experiences that might be too overwhelming to articulate verbally. Play therapy provides a safe space where children can symbolically recreate their experiences, using toys and play scenarios to explore difficult emotions and develop healthy coping mechanisms. A therapist specializing in trauma- informed care can guide this process, ensuring a supportive and therapeutic environment.

For parents, self-care is not a luxury; it's a necessity. When parents are emotionally depleted or struggling with their own unresolved trauma, they are less equipped to handle their children's challenging behaviors. Engaging in self-reflection, seeking professional support, and practicing stress- management techniques are essential. Parents need to address their own emotional needs before effectively supporting their children. Recognizing and addressing your own trauma's impact on your parenting is a crucial step in creating a healthier environment for your children. This may involve seeking therapy or engaging in self-help practices aimed at processing past experiences and developing healthier coping mechanisms.

Remember that addressing challenging behaviors in children requires a holistic approach. It's not just about managing the outward manifestations of the problem but addressing the underlying causes. Understanding the impact of intergenerational trauma, fostering secure attachment, and using effective strategies for emotional regulation and communication are crucial to breaking the cycle of trauma and helping children develop into emotionally healthy adults. The journey requires patience, empathy, and a commitment to fostering a supportive and understanding environment. The investment in time and effort is substantial, but the long-term benefits of nurturing a secure and emotionally resilient child are invaluable. Providing a safe haven where children feel accepted, understood and empowered allows them to develop healthier coping strategies, breaking free from the potentially cyclical patterns of previous generations.

This multifaceted approach includes actively seeking professional help when needed. A therapist specializing in trauma-informed care can provide valuable support and guidance, tailoring interventions to your family's unique

needs and circumstances. They can help you identify underlying issues, develop effective coping strategies, and build stronger parent-child relationships. Group therapy for parents can also provide valuable support, allowing parents to connect with others facing similar challenges and learn from shared experiences. This peer support system can significantly reduce feelings of isolation and increase overall well-being.

The impact of intergenerational trauma extends beyond immediate family dynamics, affecting societal structures and intergenerational relationships in profound ways. These influences are deeply rooted in systemic inequalities and historical injustices. Understanding and acknowledging this broader context enhances the effectiveness of our intervention strategies. It moves beyond the individual level to a deeper comprehension of the larger societal forces at play, influencing the patterns of trauma transmission across generations. By creating awareness of these systemic issues, we contribute to a larger movement towards collective healing.

Finally, remember that this journey is not a sprint, but a marathon. There will be setbacks and challenges along the way. Be kind to yourself, celebrate small victories, and never underestimate the power of patience, empathy, and consistent effort in breaking the cycle of generational trauma and fostering healthier family dynamics. The process of healing is not linear; it requires sustained effort and a commitment to self-reflection and growth. It is a journey that requires ongoing patience and perseverance, but the rewards are immeasurable, creating a lasting legacy of healthier family relationships and emotional well-being for future generations. The ultimate aim is to break free from these cycles, equipping your children with the emotional re-silience

and tools they need to navigate their own lives effectively, leading to a healthier and more fulfilling future.

Chapter 18

Addressing Anger and Frustration in Parents

The previous chapter focused on understanding and responding to your children's challenging behaviors, recognizing the potential roots in intergenerational trauma. Now, let's turn our attention inward. As parents, we are not immune to the effects of past experiences. Unresolved trauma, anxieties, and ingrained coping mechanisms can significantly impact our emotional regulation, often manifesting as anger and frustration towards our children. It's crucial to acknowledge that these feelings are not inherently "wrong," but rather indicators that we, too, need support and healing. Unmanaged anger and frustration, however, can perpetuate the cycle of trauma, harming our children and hindering their healthy development. Therefore, developing healthy ways to manage these emotions is paramount to creating a nurturing and safe environment for your family.

This is not about suppressing feelings; rather, it's about developing healthy outlets and strategies for processing them constructively. Ignoring anger or frustration only allows them to fester, eventually erupting in ways that can be damaging to your children and your relationships. The goal is to build emotional resilience, equipping yourselves with the tools to navigate difficult emotions without resorting to harmful behaviors. This process often requires self- reflection, identifying the triggers that evoke these intense emotions, and recognizing the underlying needs that may be fueling them. Are you feeling overwhelmed, stressed, or unsupported? Is there underlying unresolved trauma from your own childhood surfacing in your parenting?

Understanding these roots is crucial to addressing the symptoms.

One of the most effective strategies involves cultivating self-awareness. Begin by paying attention to your body's physical cues. What happens in your body when you start to feel angry or frustrated? Do you clench your jaw, feel your heart racing, or experience tension in your shoulders? Recognizing these physical sensations can serve as an early warning system, signaling the need to employ coping mechanisms before the emotions escalate. Keeping a journal can be incredibly helpful in this process. Record situations that trigger anger or frustration, note your physical sensations, and reflect on the underlying emotions. Over time, this self- monitoring will provide invaluable insight into your emotional patterns and trigger points.

Once you've identified your triggers and understand the underlying emotions, you can begin to develop effective coping mechanisms. These mechanisms should be tailored to your individual needs and preferences. Some effective strategies include:

Deep Breathing Exercises: Simple breathing techniques can significantly calm your nervous system, helping you regain control when feeling overwhelmed. Try inhaling deeply through your nose, holding your breath for a few seconds, and then exhaling slowly through your mouth. Repeat this several times until you feel your heart rate slowing and your tension easing. Guided meditation apps can also be helpful in learning and practicing various breathing techniques.

Mindfulness and Meditation: Mindfulness practices involve paying attention to the present moment without judgment. This can be as simple as focusing on your breath, the sensations in your body, or the sounds around you.

Regular mindfulness practice can enhance your ability to observe your emotions without getting swept away by them.

Numerous apps offer guided mindfulness meditations tailored to stress reduction and emotional regulation.

Physical Exercise: Physical activity is a powerful stress reliever. Engage in activities you enjoy, whether it's a brisk walk, a yoga session, a run, or a trip to the gym. Exercise releases endorphins, which have mood-boosting effects.

Finding an activity you enjoy will make it more likely you'll stick with it consistently.

Progressive Muscle Relaxation: This technique involves systematically tensing and relaxing different muscle groups in your body. Starting with your toes and working your way up to your head, you tense each muscle group for a few seconds, then release the tension, noticing the difference between tension and relaxation. This process can help relieve physical tension associated with anger and frustration.

Spending Time in Nature: Spending time outdoors, whether it's a walk in the park, a hike in the woods, or simply sitting under a tree, can have a calming and restorative effect. Nature's beauty and tranquility can help you reconnect with yourself and reduce stress.

Creative Expression: Expressing your emotions through creative outlets, such as painting, writing, playing music, or dancing, can be a healthy way to process anger and frustration. Art therapy, in particular, can be extremely helpful in exploring and expressing difficult emotions in a safe and supportive environment.

Seeking Social Support: Talking to a trusted friend, family member, or therapist can provide invaluable emotional support. Sharing your struggles can help reduce feelings of isolation and provide a perspective you might not have

considered on your own. Remember that seeking support is a sign of strength, not weakness.

Professional Help: If you find that you're struggling to manage your anger and frustration on your own, don't hesitate to seek professional help. A therapist can provide guidance and support in developing healthier coping mechanisms, addressing any underlying trauma, and improving your emotional regulation skills. Therapy provides a safe and confidential space to explore your emotions without judgment.

It's important to remember that these are just a few examples; the key is to find the strategies that work best for you. Experiment with different techniques and be patient with yourself. Developing healthy coping mechanisms takes time and effort. It's a journey, not a destination. Don't get discouraged if you have setbacks. Acknowledge them, learn from them, and continue to practice your chosen strategies.

Consider implementing time-outs when you feel overwhelmed. This isn't about punishing your child; it's about giving yourself the space you need to regulate your emotions before interacting with your child. Step away from the situation, take some deep breaths, and utilize your chosen coping mechanisms before returning to engage with your child calmly and rationally. Explain to your children that you need a few minutes to collect yourself and that you'll be back shortly. This teaches them healthy ways to manage their own emotions as well.

It's vital to integrate these strategies into your daily life, even when you don't feel particularly angry or frustrated. This proactive approach builds emotional resilience and strengthens your ability to respond effectively to challenging situations when they inevitably arise. Think of it as

preventative maintenance for your emotional well-being. Just as regular exercise strengthens your physical body, practicing these coping mechanisms strengthens your emotional resilience, making you better equipped to handle the inevitable stressors of parenthood.

Beyond individual coping mechanisms, consider the broader context of your life. Are you getting enough sleep? Are you eating nutritious meals? Are you engaging in regular self- care practices? Neglecting these fundamental aspects of well-being can exacerbate feelings of anger and frustration. Prioritizing your own physical and mental health is not selfish; it's essential for effective parenting. Make time for activities that nourish your soul and bring you joy. This might involve spending time with loved ones, pursuing hobbies, reading, or simply relaxing and unwinding.

Remember the ripple effect of your emotions. Your children are acutely attuned to your emotional state. When you model healthy emotional regulation, you provide them with invaluable lessons in managing their own emotions. This creates a foundation for healthier communication, stronger family bonds, and improved overall family dynamics. By addressing your own anger and frustration constructively, you break the cycle of intergenerational trauma, creating a more nurturing and supportive environment for your children and future generations.

Finally, consider seeking support from parenting groups or support networks. Sharing experiences and challenges with other parents can be incredibly validating and helpful.

Knowing you're not alone in your struggles can significantly reduce feelings of isolation and provide a sense of community and shared understanding. These groups offer opportunities to learn from other parents' experiences, share

coping strategies, and receive emotional support from peers who are navigating similar challenges.

Addressing anger and frustration isn't a one-time fix; it's an ongoing process of self-discovery, learning, and growth. It requires commitment, patience, and a willingness to prioritize your own emotional well-being. However, the rewards are immeasurable, creating a more loving, supportive, and emotionally healthy environment for your family. The journey to heal intergenerational trauma is a collaborative effort, starting with the healing and growth within yourself. By prioritizing your own emotional well- being, you empower yourselves and your children to break free from unhealthy patterns and build a brighter, healthier future for generations to come.

Chapter 19

Teaching Children Emotional Regulation Skills

Building upon the foundation of self-awareness and emotional regulation we established in the previous chapter, let's now explore how to equip our children with the same crucial life skills. Teaching children emotional regulation isn't about suppressing their feelings; instead, it's about empowering them to understand, process, and manage their emotions in healthy ways. This process, like our own journey of self-discovery, requires patience, consistency, and a deep understanding of child development.

One of the most effective strategies is to start young. Even toddlers can begin to learn about emotions. Use simple language and relatable examples. When your child is upset, instead of simply telling them to "stop crying," acknowledge their feelings. Say things like, "You seem really frustrated because your block tower fell down. That's okay to feel frustrated." This validation is key. It teaches children that their feelings are valid and worthy of attention. It also normalizes the experience of difficult emotions, preventing them from feeling shame or guilt around their feelings.

As children grow older, we can introduce more sophisticated vocabulary and concepts. Help them identify the nuances of emotions. Are they sad, angry, or frustrated? Is it a mix of emotions? Encourage them to articulate what they're feeling and why. Reading books about emotions, watching age- appropriate videos, or playing games that involve identifying facial expressions are all excellent tools to help children expand their emotional lexicon.

Role-playing is another incredibly powerful technique. You can create scenarios together where you act out different

emotional responses to challenging situations. For example, imagine your child is struggling to share a toy. You can role- play both sides of the conflict – the child who wants the toy and the child who has the toy. Discuss various responses, exploring both constructive and destructive approaches. This allows children to see the consequences of different actions and learn to choose more appropriate responses in real-life situations.

Creating a safe space for children to express their emotions is paramount. This involves active listening without judgment. Avoid dismissing their feelings as trivial or telling them to "be strong." Instead, show empathy and understanding. Let them know that it's okay to feel whatever they're feeling, even if it's anger, sadness, or fear. This creates a secure attachment, fostering a sense of trust and encouraging open communication.

Teaching children coping mechanisms is another vital step in their emotional development. These mechanisms should be age-appropriate and tailored to their individual needs and personalities. For younger children, simple activities like deep breathing exercises, counting to ten, or squeezing a stress ball can be effective. For older children, you might explore journaling, mindfulness practices, creative expression through art or music, or engaging in physical activity like running or sports.

The goal is to equip them with a toolkit of strategies they can access when they feel overwhelmed.

It's crucial to model healthy emotional regulation ourselves. Children learn by observing and imitating. If they see us managing our own emotions constructively, they are more likely to adopt similar strategies. This includes acknowledging our own struggles and sharing our own coping mechanisms with them, demonstrating vulnerability

in a healthy way. This transparency builds trust and shows children that it's okay to not be perfect; everyone has challenges to navigate.

Consistency is key. Teaching emotional regulation is not a one-time event; it's an ongoing process that requires consistent reinforcement. It's about weaving emotional literacy into the fabric of our daily interactions. Praise and encourage their efforts, even when they stumble. Remember that setbacks are a normal part of the learning process.

Celebrate their successes, both big and small, reinforcing the positive behaviors and strengthening their confidence in their ability to manage their emotions.

Beyond individual strategies, building a strong family support system is vital. Family meetings, where everyone can openly share their feelings and concerns, can be invaluable. This fosters a sense of community and mutual support, teaching children that they're not alone in their struggles. Creating family rituals, such as regular game nights or family dinners, can help strengthen family bonds and provide a sense of stability and predictability, both of which contribute significantly to emotional well-being.

Furthermore, seeking professional guidance when necessary is a sign of strength, not weakness. If you're struggling to manage your own emotions or to help your child regulate theirs, consider seeking support from a therapist or counselor. They can provide personalized strategies and support, helping you navigate challenges and build stronger family relationships. They can also assess for underlying issues, such as anxiety or trauma, that might be contributing to emotional difficulties. Don't hesitate to reach out for help; it's a testament to your commitment to your child's well- being and your own.

In addition to the techniques mentioned earlier, consider incorporating elements of mindfulness into your child's life. Mindfulness, often associated with meditation, is the practice of being present in the moment, observing thoughts and feelings without judgment. For children, this might involve simple exercises such as focusing on their breath, noticing sensations in their body, or paying close attention to their surroundings. Mindfulness helps children develop a sense of self-awareness and the ability to observe their emotions without getting swept away by them.

For younger children, mindfulness can be incorporated through playful activities. For example, you can engage them in a "body scan" where they slowly bring awareness to different parts of their body, noticing any sensations. Or you can encourage them to pay close attention to the sounds, smells, and sights around them during a nature walk. These activities foster present moment awareness and can be a valuable tool in helping children manage stress and anxiety.

Storytelling can also be a powerful tool for teaching emotional regulation. Stories that feature characters dealing with challenging emotions, such as anger, fear, or sadness, offer children a safe space to explore these feelings vicariously. Discuss the characters' feelings and the strategies they use to cope. This provides a framework for children to understand and process their own emotions and learn from others' experiences.

Visual aids, such as emotion charts or flashcards, can be helpful, especially for younger children. These visual representations can help children identify and label their emotions, and they can serve as a reminder of coping strategies when they are feeling overwhelmed. You can create your own emotion chart together, making it a collaborative and personalized tool.

Remember, consistency and patience are essential when teaching children emotional regulation. It's a gradual process that requires repeated practice and reinforcement. Celebrate their progress and encourage them to persevere even when they struggle. Create a supportive and understanding environment where they feel safe expressing their feelings without fear of judgment.

Finally, consider involving your child in the process of developing coping strategies. Ask them what they think would help them when they are feeling upset. This empowers them and demonstrates respect for their experience. By involving them in the decision-making process, you foster a sense of ownership and increase the likelihood of them utilizing the strategies you've developed together. This collaborative approach promotes a positive and supportive relationship, strengthening your bond and building their confidence in managing their own emotions effectively. This empowers them to navigate life's challenges with resilience and emotional intelligence, fostering a stronger sense of self and contributing to their overall well-being. Remember, the goal is not to eliminate difficult emotions, but rather to empower children to manage them in healthy, constructive ways, breaking the cycle of intergenerational trauma and fostering a happier, healthier future for generations to come.

Seeking External Support for Conflict Resolution

Building on the strategies for managing conflict within the family unit, we now turn to the crucial consideration of when and how to seek external support. While open communication and proactive conflict resolution techniques are invaluable, some family conflicts are too deeply entrenched, too complex, or too emotionally charged to navigate successfully without professional guidance.

Recognizing the limitations of our own abilities and seeking help is not a sign of weakness, but rather a testament to our commitment to fostering healthy family relationships.

The decision to seek professional help should not be taken lightly, but neither should it be delayed when the need is clear. There are numerous red flags that might indicate the necessity of professional intervention. Persistent, unresolved conflicts that significantly impact the well-being of family members are a strong indicator. This might manifest as ongoing arguments, escalating tension, emotional distancing, or a pervasive sense of unhappiness within the family dynamic. Observe the impact on individual family members – is anyone experiencing significant anxiety, depression, or exhibiting unhealthy coping mechanisms like substance abuse, self-harm, or withdrawal? These are critical signs that professional help is needed.

Consider the nature of the conflict itself. Is it rooted in deep-seated trauma or unresolved grief? Does it involve complex issues like abuse, neglect, addiction, or betrayal? These situations often require specialized expertise to address the underlying causes and facilitate healing. Trying to navigate such complexities independently can be counterproductive and even harmful. Remember, you don't have to bear the weight of these challenges alone.

Another important factor is the family's capacity for self- regulation and problem-solving. Are attempts at communication repeatedly failing? Are family members unable to engage in constructive dialogue or compromise? If attempts at implementing the strategies discussed in previous chapters repeatedly prove ineffective, seeking professional help may be necessary to facilitate a shift in communication patterns and conflict resolution approaches. A neutral third party can provide the structure and guidance needed to break through ingrained patterns and establish healthier ways of interacting.

The type of professional support you seek will depend on the specific needs of your family. Family therapy, offered by licensed therapists or counselors specializing in family systems, provides a structured environment for family members to address their conflicts directly, learn communication skills, and develop healthier interaction patterns. A therapist can help identify dysfunctional patterns, facilitate open communication, and guide the family toward constructive solutions. The therapist acts as a facilitator, not a judge, creating a safe space for vulnerability and honest expression. They can help family members understand each other's perspectives, even when those perspectives are vastly different or rooted in painful experiences.

If trauma is a significant factor in your family's conflicts, consider seeking a therapist specializing in trauma-informed care. Trauma-informed therapy acknowledges the profound impact of past experiences and emphasizes creating a safe and supportive environment where individuals can process their trauma at their own pace. This approach avoids

triggering or re-traumatizing individuals and focuses on building resilience and fostering emotional regulation.

In situations involving severe conflict, such as domestic violence or child abuse, it's crucial to prioritize safety. Reach out to the appropriate authorities – law enforcement, child protective services, or domestic violence shelters – to ensure the safety and well-being of all family members.

Professional intervention in such circumstances is not just advisable, it is essential.

Choosing the right therapist is a critical step. Consider their experience, qualifications, and approach. Look for a therapist who specializes in family therapy and has experience working with families facing similar challenges. Some therapists have expertise in specific areas, such as trauma, addiction, or grief and loss. It's important to feel comfortable and safe with your therapist, so don't hesitate to interview several professionals before selecting one. A good therapist will listen attentively, show empathy, and create a collaborative partnership with your family.

The initial therapy sessions often involve assessment, where the therapist gathers information about the family's history, dynamics, and current challenges. This might involve individual sessions, as well as family sessions. The therapist will help family members identify their roles in the conflicts, explore underlying issues, and develop strategies for healthier communication. Throughout the therapy process, the therapist will provide feedback, guidance, and support, helping family members learn to manage their emotions, resolve disagreements constructively, and build stronger, healthier relationships.

The duration of therapy will vary depending on the complexity of the issues and the family's progress. Some

families benefit from short-term therapy, focused on addressing specific conflicts, while others may require longer-term therapy to address deep-seated issues and facilitate lasting change. Remember, therapy is a journey, not a quick fix. Progress may be gradual, with setbacks along the way. Consistency and commitment are key to achieving positive outcomes.

Beyond family therapy, other forms of external support can also be beneficial. Support groups, whether for parents, children, or individuals struggling with specific issues, provide a sense of community and shared understanding.

These groups offer a space to connect with others facing similar challenges, share experiences, and learn from one another. The support of peers can be incredibly powerful in navigating difficult family situations. Similarly, individual therapy can be helpful for individual family members struggling with specific emotional or mental health challenges. Addressing individual issues can significantly improve the overall functioning of the family system.

Mediation is another option, particularly in situations involving high-conflict divorce or inheritance disputes. A trained mediator helps family members communicate more effectively, explore solutions collaboratively, and reach mutually agreeable outcomes. Mediation is often more cost- effective and less emotionally draining than protracted legal battles.

The decision to seek external support is a courageous step toward building a healthier family. It demonstrates a commitment to positive change and a willingness to invest in the well-being of all family members. While it may feel challenging initially, the rewards of healing, improved communication, and stronger family bonds are immeasurable. Remember, seeking help is not a sign of

failure, but a sign of strength and resilience. It is an act of hope and a commitment to breaking the cycles of intergenerational trauma and building a healthier future for your family. The journey towards healing is often challenging, but the potential for positive transformation is significant, creating a ripple effect of positive change for generations to come. By proactively addressing family conflicts and seeking professional help when needed, you are laying the foundation for a more harmonious and resilient family for the future. This investment in your family's well- being will have a profound and lasting positive effect, fostering stronger connections, healthier relationships, and greater overall well-being for everyone involved. By embracing the opportunity to heal, to grow, and to build a more loving and supportive family dynamic, you are demonstrating a commitment not only to your immediate family but to generations to come. The cycle of intergenerational trauma can be broken through conscious effort, open communication, and the willingness to seek help when needed. Remember, you are not alone in this journey.

Support is available, and by actively engaging in the process of healing, you are creating a brighter future for your family. This commitment to your family's well-being is a testament to the strength of your love and your dedication to creating a healthy family dynamic where every member can thrive.

Take heart in the steps you are taking and know that your efforts will have a positive and lasting impact on the lives of those you love.

Chapter 20

Building Emotional Resilience in Children

Building emotional resilience in children is not about shielding them from hardship; it's about equipping them with the tools to navigate life's inevitable challenges. It's about fostering a sense of self-efficacy – the belief in their ability to overcome obstacles and bounce back from adversity. This involves nurturing their emotional intelligence, teaching them healthy coping mechanisms, and creating a supportive environment where they feel safe to express their feelings and seek help when needed. Children who develop strong emotional resilience are better equipped to handle stress, anxiety, and setbacks, leading to greater overall well-being and success in life.

One of the cornerstones of emotional resilience is the development of strong self-esteem. Children with high self- esteem believe in their worth and capabilities, even when faced with difficulties. This self-belief acts as a buffer against negativity and helps them persevere through challenges. Parents can foster self-esteem by providing unconditional love and acceptance. This doesn't mean condoning negative behaviors, but rather, consistently conveying the message that their child is valued and loved regardless of their mistakes or achievements. Positive reinforcement, focusing on effort and progress rather than solely on outcomes, is crucial. Praising a child's persistence in completing a difficult task, for instance, is more effective than solely focusing on the final result. Regularly offering specific and genuine praise strengthens their sense of self- worth. Avoid making comparisons with siblings or peers; every child develops at their own pace and has their unique strengths.

Beyond positive reinforcement, actively encouraging self-compassion is vital. Children, just like adults, make mistakes and experience setbacks. Teaching them to treat themselves with the same kindness and understanding they would offer a friend facing similar challenges is a powerful resilience- building skill. Encourage them to reflect on their mistakes without self-criticism, focusing instead on what they can learn from the experience. Help them reframe negative self- talk, replacing self-deprecating statements with positive affirmations. For instance, if a child says "I'm so stupid, I failed that test," guide them to reframe it as "I didn't do as well as I hoped on that test, but I can learn from my mistakes and study harder next time."

Another key element in fostering emotional resilience is teaching children effective coping mechanisms. This involves equipping them with a range of strategies to manage stress, anxiety, and difficult emotions. These strategies can be both cognitive and behavioral. Cognitive strategies involve changing the way children think about stressful situations. For example, teaching them to identify and challenge negative thoughts, replacing them with more positive and realistic ones, is crucial. Behavioral strategies involve changing the way children react to stressful situations. This might involve teaching relaxation techniques such as deep breathing exercises, progressive muscle relaxation, or mindfulness meditation. These techniques can help children calm down and regulate their emotions when feeling overwhelmed. Incorporating physical activity, such as regular exercise or playing sports, is also immensely beneficial in managing stress and improving overall mood.

Regular family time dedicated to shared activities strengthens family bonds and provides a safe and supportive environment for emotional expression. These activities don't need to be elaborate; they can be simple things like playing

board games, reading together, having family dinners, or going for walks in nature. The key is to create opportunities for positive interaction and connection. These shared experiences foster a sense of belonging and security, creating a safe haven for children to express their emotions and seek comfort when needed. During these times, active listening is essential. Children need to feel heard and understood, even when their feelings seem unreasonable to adults. Validation of their emotions, even if you don't necessarily agree with their perspective, shows them that their feelings are important and worthy of consideration.

Teaching children problem-solving skills is another important aspect of building emotional resilience. This involves guiding them through a structured process to identify problems, brainstorm solutions, evaluate options, and implement a chosen solution. Start with simple scenarios, gradually increasing the complexity as their skills improve. For example, help a child resolve a conflict with a sibling by teaching them how to express their feelings calmly and respectfully, negotiate compromises, and find mutually acceptable solutions. These problem-solving skills translate to various aspects of life, empowering children to tackle challenges independently.

Mindfulness and gratitude practices offer further support for emotional well-being. Mindfulness teaches children to focus on the present moment, reducing rumination on past events or anxieties about the future. Simple mindfulness exercises, like paying attention to their breath or focusing on their senses during a shared activity, can be incorporated into daily routines. Practicing gratitude, by regularly acknowledging positive aspects of their lives, promotes positivity and optimism. Encouraging children to keep a gratitude journal, where they write down things they are thankful for each day, can foster this practice. These habits

create a positive feedback loop, strengthening their resilience against negative influences.

The role of modelling appropriate emotional regulation is paramount. Children learn by observing their parents and caregivers. Therefore, parents need to demonstrate healthy coping mechanisms and emotional regulation in their own lives. Openly expressing feelings appropriately, managing conflict constructively, and seeking support when needed, all serve as powerful examples for children to emulate.

Acknowledging your own struggles and demonstrating how you navigate them is more effective than trying to appear perfect. Children learn that it's okay to struggle and that seeking help is a sign of strength, not weakness.

Building emotional resilience is an ongoing process, requiring consistent effort and support. By nurturing self- esteem, teaching healthy coping mechanisms, fostering strong family bonds, and modelling appropriate emotional regulation, parents can equip their children with the essential tools to thrive in the face of adversity. The journey isn't about eliminating hardship but about empowering children to navigate life's challenges with confidence and resilience, paving the way for a more fulfilling and successful future.

Remember to celebrate small victories and progress, acknowledging the ongoing effort and dedication involved in this crucial aspect of child development. The investment in fostering resilience pays dividends, not only for the child but for the entire family, building a foundation of strength and well-being for generations to come. This journey of building resilience is not just about the child's growth; it's about fostering a healthier, more emotionally intelligent family dynamic where support, understanding and mutual respect are the cornerstones of a thriving familial unit. The work required is a collaborative effort where parent and child learn, grow, and adapt together.

Promoting SelfEsteem and SelfConfidence

Building a child's self-esteem and self-confidence is a cornerstone of fostering resilience. It's not about inflated praise or unrealistic expectations, but about providing a consistent foundation of genuine affirmation and support. This involves actively noticing and celebrating their efforts, even small ones. A child who diligently completes a challenging puzzle, even if it takes them a long time, deserves praise for their perseverance, not just for the final outcome. Similarly, acknowledging their emotional efforts – expressing their feelings appropriately, handling frustration constructively – reinforces their developing self-awareness and emotional intelligence. Focusing on the process rather than solely on the product cultivates a growth mindset, where challenges are seen as opportunities for learning and development rather than indicators of failure.

Positive reinforcement isn't just about verbal praise. It can also involve nonverbal cues – a warm smile, a reassuring touch, a knowing nod of approval. These small gestures can communicate acceptance and understanding far more powerfully than words alone. Actively listening to their concerns, offering validation for their feelings, and acknowledging their perspective, even if you don't agree with it, demonstrates respect and creates a safe space for open communication. This openness fosters a secure attachment, crucial for developing a healthy sense of self. A child who feels heard and understood is more likely to trust their own judgment and develop a strong sense of self-worth.

Furthermore, encouraging children to identify and celebrate their own strengths is paramount. What are they good at?

What do they enjoy? Helping them articulate these qualities empowers them to recognize their inherent value and capabilities. This self-discovery is a lifelong process that should be nurtured from a young age. Regularly asking questions like "What was your favorite part of today?" or "What are you proud of accomplishing?" prompts reflection and self-awareness. Encourage them to participate in activities that challenge them appropriately, pushing them beyond their comfort zone in a safe and supportive environment. This helps them build resilience through facing challenges and experiencing success.

Creating opportunities for children to experience mastery is also vital. This doesn't mean setting them up for guaranteed success, but rather providing appropriate challenges that are neither too easy nor too difficult. When a child experiences the satisfaction of overcoming a challenge, they develop a sense of competence and self-efficacy – the belief in their ability to achieve their goals. This belief is the bedrock of self-confidence. Breaking down larger tasks into smaller, more manageable steps can help children feel a sense of accomplishment along the way, building momentum and maintaining motivation. Celebrating milestones, however small, reinforces their progress and encourages them to persevere.

However, fostering self-esteem is not about avoiding challenges or shielding children from disappointment. In fact, navigating setbacks is crucial for building resilience. The goal isn't to eliminate adversity, but to equip children with the emotional tools and coping strategies to handle it effectively. When children experience disappointment or failure, it's an opportunity to model healthy coping mechanisms and emotional regulation. Parents can demonstrate empathy and understanding while simultaneously guiding the child in problem-solving and finding constructive ways to address the situation. Helping

them reframe setbacks as learning opportunities and emphasizing the importance of persistence is crucial. It's essential to reinforce the idea that mistakes are inevitable and that they are opportunities for growth, not evidence of inadequacy.

The importance of role modeling cannot be overstated. Children learn by observing the behaviors and attitudes of the adults in their lives. Parents who demonstrate self-esteem and self-confidence, who handle challenges with grace and resilience, are providing invaluable role models for their children. This includes open expression of emotions, healthy conflict resolution, and positive self-talk. Children observe how parents manage their own feelings and react to setbacks. Modeling healthy coping mechanisms provides children with valuable tools and strategies for their own lives. It shows them that setbacks are temporary, and that perseverance and self-belief are key to overcoming challenges. Parents demonstrating healthy self-esteem and emotional regulation are in effect, providing a living demonstration of resilience to their children. This implicit learning is often as powerful, if not more so, than explicit instruction.

Another crucial aspect of building self-esteem is fostering a sense of belonging. Children need to feel loved, accepted, and valued for who they are, regardless of their accomplishments. This involves creating a warm and supportive family environment where they feel safe to express their individuality and pursue their interests.

Encouraging participation in activities that foster social interaction and collaboration, like team sports or community service projects, helps build social skills and a sense of connection with others. Belonging to a group, feeling understood and valued by peers, contributes significantly to self-esteem and self-confidence. This sense of belonging is not limited to the family unit; it also extends to a child's

wider social network, including friends, teachers, and other influential adults in their lives.

Furthermore, promoting healthy self-care practices is vital for both parents and children. Self-care is not a luxury; it's a necessity, especially in the face of stress and adversity. It's about prioritizing activities that support physical and emotional well-being. This could include regular exercise, healthy eating, sufficient sleep, and engaging in enjoyable hobbies. Modeling self-care practices sets a positive example for children and underscores the importance of prioritizing their own well-being. When parents prioritize their own mental and physical health, they create a more nurturing and supportive environment for their children. This creates a cycle of well-being, where both parents and children benefit from prioritizing self-care.

However, it's important to avoid falling into the trap of conditional self-esteem. This is where a child's self-worth is contingent upon their achievements or external validation.

Instead, foster unconditional positive regard – a deep and abiding love and acceptance that is independent of their performance or behavior. This means loving and accepting them for who they are, even when they make mistakes or face challenges. It's about emphasizing their inherent worth as individuals, regardless of their accomplishments. This unconditional love and acceptance provides a solid foundation for self-esteem, allowing them to navigate life's ups and downs with greater confidence and resilience.

It's crucial to remember that building self-esteem is a gradual and ongoing process. It requires consistent effort, patience, and understanding. There will be setbacks and challenges along the way, but the rewards of nurturing a child's self- worth are im-measurable. A child with strong self-esteem is more likely to be resilient, adaptable, and successful in life.

They are better equipped to handle stress, overcome adversity, and build positive relationships. Ultimately, fostering self-esteem is an investment in the child's future well-being and contributes to creating a more resilient and emotionally intelligent family unit. The process requires collaboration between parents and children, creating a supportive environment where both learn and grow together. The ongoing effort invested in nurturing self-esteem strengthens family bonds and fosters a cycle of resilience that extends across generations.

Chapter 21

The Importance of Play and Fun

Building a child's resilience extends beyond fostering self-esteem and self-confidence; it thrives in the fertile ground of shared joy and playful connection. Play isn't just a frivolous pastime; it's a fundamental human need, particularly crucial for children navigating the complexities of life and the echoes of intergenerational trauma. Engaging in playful activities strengthens family bonds, fosters emotional regulation, and builds resilience in ways that structured interactions often can't. Shared laughter, spontaneous games, and collaborative creativity forge deeper connections, creating a safe haven where vulnerability is embraced and healing can occur. The act of playful engagement itself becomes a powerful tool for emotional regulation, offering a release valve for stress and anxiety, helping children (and parents) process emotions constructively. When families laugh together, they build resilience as a unit, strengthening their capacity to weather life's storms. The memories forged during these playful moments become anchors in times of difficulty, offering a sense of stability and comfort.

The importance of play extends beyond simple amusement; it's a potent vehicle for learning crucial life skills. Through imaginative play, children develop problem-solving abilities, learn to negotiate and compromise, and practice emotional expression in a safe environment. Building a tower of blocks teaches patience, perseverance, and the acceptance of setbacks. Playing a board game fosters strategic thinking, cooperation, and healthy competition. Even seemingly simple activities like drawing, singing, or dancing offer opportunities for self-expression, creativity, and the exploration of emotions. These playful interactions model healthy coping mechanisms, teaching children how to

regulate their emotions, manage frustration, and resolve conflicts constructively. Parents who participate actively in these activities not only strengthen their bond with their children but also demonstrate healthy emotional processing, indirectly teaching their children by example. This modeling of coping strategies is often more impactful than any lecture or directive.

Furthermore, play provides a crucial avenue for communication that transcends the barriers often erected in more formal settings. During play, the focus shifts from lecturing or instructing to shared experience, creating a sense of equality and camaraderie that fosters open communication. Children are more likely to express their fears, anxieties, and vulnerabilities during play, making it an invaluable tool for parents to understand their child's emotional landscape. This understanding is crucial in providing appropriate support and guidance, particularly in families dealing with the complex dynamics of intergenerational trauma. Play offers an unobstructed pathway for parents to connect with their children on a deeper, more emotional level, fostering a sense of trust and safety that is essential for healing. Observing a child's interactions during play can provide insights into their emotional state, their coping mechanisms, and their understanding of the world around them, offering valuable clues about any unresolved traumas that may be manifesting.

The type of play doesn't need to be elaborate or expensive. Simple, everyday activities can be incredibly powerful. A game of catch in the park, a family dance party in the living room, or a collaborative baking session can all create lasting positive memories and strengthen family bonds. The key is active participation and shared enjoyment. Even bedtime stories, though not strictly "play," serve a similar purpose, fostering a connection through shared imagination and

emotional intimacy. The narrative structure of stories allows for the exploration of complex emotions and challenging situations in a safe and indirect way, providing opportunities for conversation and emotional processing. Choosing stories that reflect the family's cultural background or address themes of resilience and overcoming adversity can further reinforce positive messages and contribute to the healing process.

However, the challenge lies in consciously incorporating play into busy family schedules. Many families struggle to find time for these seemingly "unproductive" activities, prioritizing structured activities and academic achievements. This prioritization often stems from societal pressures and the pervasive belief that structured learning is the sole pathway to success. However, prioritizing play is not counterproductive; it's a vital component of a child's overall development and well-being. It's an investment in their emotional health, resilience, and future success. Parents who consciously carve out time for play are not only investing in their child's development but also fostering stronger family bonds and cultivating a more resilient and joyful family unit. This prioritization of play, particularly in families burdened by generational trauma, becomes a significant step towards breaking the cycle of negative patterns and fostering healthier intergenerational relationships.

Integrating play into the family routine requires conscious effort and planning. This doesn't necessarily involve significant changes to existing schedules, but rather a mindful shift in perspective. Even short bursts of playful interaction throughout the day can be incredibly effective. A few minutes of silly faces during breakfast, a spontaneous tickle fight after homework, or a shared game of cards before bedtime can all contribute to a sense of connection and joy.

It is crucial for parents to actively participate in these

activities, demonstrating their commitment to play and enjoyment. This active participation models the importance of play and reinforces the message that it is valued and appreciated within the family. Children learn by observing their parents' behavior; modeling a playful and joyful approach to life teaches children to embrace play as a positive and constructive activity.

Moreover, the benefits of play extend to parents as well. Engaging in playful interactions with their children provides parents with an opportunity to de-stress, reconnect with their own inner child, and experience the joy of shared laughter.

This is particularly beneficial for parents struggling with the effects of their own childhood traumas. Engaging in playful interactions can be a form of self-care, providing a break from the stressors of daily life and fostering a sense of emotional well-being. Play offers a natural pathway for emotional regulation, allowing parents to process their emotions in a healthy and constructive manner. This emotional regulation is vital for parents navigating the complexities of intergenerational trauma; when parents are able to regulate their emotions effectively, they are better equipped to provide support and guidance to their children.

Furthermore, incorporating different types of play can cater to various developmental needs and preferences. For younger children, sensory play, such as playing with sand, water, or play-dough, can stimulate development and encourage creativity. For older children, board games, card games, or sports can foster social skills, strategic thinking, and physical activity. For adolescents, engaging in creative activities such as drawing, music, or writing can provide outlets for self-expression and emotional processing. Parents should strive to find activities that resonate with their child's interests and personality, ensuring that play is enjoyable and engaging for everyone. This adaptability in selecting playful

activities demonstrates flexibility and responsiveness to the child's needs, further strengthening the parent-child bond.

The effort invested in finding mutually enjoyable activities underscores the parents' willingness to participate fully in their child's world, building trust and mutual understanding.

Beyond structured play, fostering spontaneity and improvisation is crucial. Creating opportunities for unplanned fun, like a surprise picnic in the backyard or a spontaneous dance-off in the living room, can inject joy and laughter into the daily routine, creating opportunities for genuine connection and strengthening family bonds. These unscheduled moments of play often hold the most potent impact, creating lasting memories and fostering a sense of shared experience. The spontaneity fosters a sense of freedom and creativity, allowing for genuine expressions of joy and connection. These unpredictable moments create a sense of excitement and anticipation, reinforcing the value of shared experience and fostering stronger family bonds.

The importance of play and shared activities extends beyond the immediate benefits for individuals; it represents a conscious effort to break the cycle of intergenerational trauma. By prioritizing play and fostering joyful family interactions, parents are actively creating a healthier and more resilient family environment. This positive environment is vital for children to develop healthy coping mechanisms, emotional intelligence, and strong self-esteem. By engaging in playful activities, families can create a safe space where emotions are processed constructively and healing can occur. This creates a foundation of resilience that will serve them well throughout their lives. The conscious act of prioritizing play stands as a powerful antidote to the negative patterns of intergenerational trauma. It represents a shift in mindset and priorities, emphasizing the importance of emotional well-being and healthy family relationships.

Play becomes a vehicle for healing and a catalyst for a brighter future.

Creating Family Rituals and Traditions

Building upon the foundation of playful connection and shared joy, we now delve into the powerful role of family rituals and traditions in fostering resilience and a strong sense of belonging. These aren't merely quaint customs; they are the bedrock upon which a resilient family structure is built. They provide a sense of continuity, predictability, and shared identity, all crucial elements in navigating the complexities of life and the lingering shadows of intergenerational trauma. Rituals and traditions offer a consistent framework, a comforting rhythm in the often chaotic flow of daily life. They create a shared narrative, a sense of "us" that transcends individual struggles and strengthens the family bond. This shared history, woven through repeated actions and shared experiences, provides a sense of security and stability, particularly vital for children who may be grappling with the inherited anxieties or unresolved issues of previous generations. The predictability they offer can be incredibly soothing, countering the instability that often accompanies intergenerational trauma. These practices become anchors, offering a sense of normalcy and grounding amidst life's inevitable storms.

They are a tangible manifestation of love, commitment, and shared identity, acting as a powerful buffer against the negative impacts of past trauma. The simple act of participating in a shared ritual can be profoundly healing, providing a space for connection, emotional regulation, and the strengthening of family bonds.

The power of family rituals lies in their ability to create a sense of belonging. When family members participate in shared activities, they are actively creating a sense of community and connection. This sense of belonging is

crucial for children, particularly those who may be struggling with feelings of isolation or insecurity due to intergenerational trauma. A strong sense of belonging provides a sense of safety and security, knowing that they are loved and accepted for who they are. Rituals foster a feeling of being valued and seen, reducing feelings of alienation and fostering a more supportive family dynamic. This is especially crucial in families grappling with the lingering effects of trauma, as feelings of isolation and disconnection often compound the difficulties. The consistent practice of family rituals counters this isolation, providing a regular opportunity for connection and interaction within a safe and predictable environment. Children who participate in meaningful family rituals often develop stronger self-esteem and a sense of identity, feeling a stronger sense of security and belonging within the family structure.

Consider the impact of a weekly family dinner. It's more than just a meal; it's an opportunity for shared conversation, laughter, and connection. In families affected by trauma, this might be a space to address difficult topics with empathy and understanding, or simply to enjoy each other's company without the weight of unresolved issues. The simple act of sitting together, sharing a meal, and engaging in conversation allows for emotional regulation and stress reduction for all family members. Similarly, bedtime stories, even for older children, can create a space for emotional connection and intimacy. These stories become a shared experience, fostering a sense of closeness and security. The repetition and ritualistic nature of this activity provide a sense of comfort and stability, acting as a counterpoint to any potential anxieties or disturbances. The power of these simple rituals lies in their consistency and predictability, providing a sense of stability and security. They are not just about the specific activity itself, but about the consistent commitment to shared time and connection.

The creation of new rituals and traditions is an opportunity for healing and growth within a family. This active engagement in building shared experiences is a key step in counteracting the negative impact of generational trauma. It's about consciously creating positive experiences that become anchors of strength and belonging. The process itself can be therapeutic, as families work together to choose activities that resonate with them, and in the process, strengthen their bond and understanding of each other's needs and desires.

This collaborative effort fosters a sense of shared responsibility and accomplishment, contributing to the overall sense of resilience within the family unit. The creation of new traditions can also help to break unhealthy patterns passed down through generations. By consciously choosing positive and healthy activities, families can actively work towards creating a more supportive and nurturing environment. This active creation of positive experiences can be particularly powerful in breaking negative patterns, demonstrating a conscious effort to create a more positive and healthy family dynamic.

Involving children in the creation of family rituals is crucial. This fosters a sense of ownership and investment in the family's traditions, further enhancing the sense of belonging and shared identity. Their participation should not be tokenistic; rather, their input should be genuinely valued and incorporated into the design and implementation of the rituals. This fosters creativity, responsibility, and collaboration within the family unit. This process is a testament to the healing power of active participation in family traditions; it is an opportunity to create something new together, while fostering a sense of collaboration, creativity, and empowerment. When children participate actively in shaping their family's traditions, they internalize these values, developing a stronger sense of belonging and

personal responsibility. This active participation provides them with a sense of agency and control, which can be especially beneficial for children who may have previously felt powerless in the face of inherited trauma.

The choice of rituals and traditions should be tailored to the specific needs and interests of the family. There's no one- size-fits-all approach; the key is to select activities that resonate with all family members, fostering a sense of shared enjoyment and connection. This personalized approach helps ensure that these practices become a source of genuine joy and connection, rather than another obligation. This personalized approach ensures that the family traditions truly reflect the unique dynamic and personality of the family. It's about creating rituals that genuinely resonate with everyone, fostering a sense of authenticity and engagement. Consider families with diverse cultural backgrounds; they may incorporate elements of their heritage into their family traditions, enriching the experience and fostering a sense of pride and continuity. Similarly, families with diverse interests might weave those interests into their family rituals. A family passionate about hiking might establish a weekly hike as a family ritual; a family with a love for music might have regular family singalongs. This personalized approach ensures that the rituals are meaningful and engaging for all family members, contributing to a stronger sense of shared identity and belonging.

The consistency of family rituals is vital to their effectiveness. Regular practice reinforces the sense of routine, predictability, and belonging. While life inevitably presents challenges that may disrupt established routines, making a conscious effort to maintain these practices is crucial. Even small, consistent actions can have a powerful cumulative effect, fostering a sense of stability and resilience. Families should aim for consistency in the

execution of their family rituals, prioritizing these traditions as much as possible, even when facing life's challenges. It's not about perfection, but about commitment and consistency. The act of actively trying to maintain these practices in the face of adversity reinforces the value and importance of family connections, demonstrating the family's commitment to building resilience together.

Beyond the emotional benefits, family rituals and traditions also contribute to the development of essential life skills.

Children learn about cooperation, teamwork, and conflict resolution as they participate in shared activities. They learn to negotiate, compromise, and express their needs in a constructive manner. These skills extend beyond the family setting, empowering them to navigate social interactions and challenges more effectively in their wider lives. This is especially beneficial in breaking the cycle of intergenerational trauma, as children learn healthy coping mechanisms and communication styles, replacing potentially harmful patterns. The act of participating in family traditions also builds resilience by strengthening family bonds and creating a shared history. These shared experiences serve as anchors in times of stress or adversity, providing a sense of stability and security. The memories created through shared traditions become resources to draw upon when facing life's inevitable challenges, providing comfort and support. These shared experiences create a strong foundation for the family to weather life's storms, drawing strength from their shared history and commitment to each other.

In conclusion, creating and maintaining family rituals and traditions is not just a charming addition to family life; it's a vital component in fostering resilience and well-being, especially for families grappling with the legacy of intergenerational trauma. These shared experiences, steeped in consistency and personalized meaning, create a powerful

sense of belonging, continuity, and shared identity, equipping family members with the emotional resources to navigate life's challenges and build a stronger, healthier future together. By consciously choosing positive experiences and actively involving everyone in the process, families can break free from unhealthy patterns, create a supportive and nurturing environment, and build resilience that will serve them well for generations to come. The effort invested in creating these shared traditions is an investment in the overall well-being and happiness of the family, creating a legacy of love, connection, and resilience that will endure for years to come. The power of these traditions extends beyond the immediate benefits; they become a lasting legacy, shaping future generations and contributing to a healthier and more fulfilling family experience for years to come. It is a powerful investment in the well-being and happiness of the family.

Chapter 22

Practicing Gratitude and Mindfulness

Building on the strength and stability established through consistent family rituals and traditions, we now turn our attention to cultivating inner resilience within the family unit. This involves nurturing individual well-being, which in turn strengthens the entire family system. A powerful approach to achieving this is through the integration of gratitude and mindfulness practices. These aren't merely feel-good exercises; they are potent tools for shifting perspectives, managing stress, and fostering emotional regulation – all crucial elements in breaking free from the cyclical patterns of intergenerational trauma.

Gratitude, the simple act of acknowledging and appreciating the positive aspects of our lives, possesses a remarkable capacity to reshape our emotional landscape. When we focus on what we have rather than what we lack, we shift our attention away from the negativity and anxieties that often accompany unresolved trauma. This isn't about ignoring challenges; it's about acknowledging both the good and the bad, fostering a more balanced perspective. For families grappling with the legacy of trauma, this balanced perspective is particularly crucial. The constant replay of past hurts and anxieties can cast a long shadow, obscuring the present joys and successes. Gratitude acts as a powerful antidote, illuminating the positive aspects of family life, strengthening bonds, and fostering a sense of hope.

Incorporating gratitude practices into family life can take many forms. A simple nightly ritual of sharing three things each family member is grateful for can create a powerful shared experience. This can be adapted to suit different age groups; young children might express gratitude for a specific

toy or a fun activity, while older children and adults might reflect on more complex aspects of their lives, such as supportive relationships or personal achievements. The key is to make it a consistent, shared experience, fostering a sense of connection and appreciation. This regular expression of gratitude can transform family interactions, turning dinner time or bedtime into opportunities for strengthening bonds and expressing appreciation.

Beyond the nightly ritual, gratitude can be woven into the fabric of everyday life. A simple "thank you" expressed sincerely can have a profound impact. Actively acknowledging and appreciating the contributions of each family member fosters a sense of belonging and validation, particularly vital for those who may feel unseen or unheard due to past traumas. Expressing gratitude for the small everyday acts of kindness and support builds a positive feedback loop, reinforcing positive interactions and creating a more nurturing family environment. This conscious act of appreciation can also foster a deeper understanding and empathy between family members, contributing to a healthier and more supportive family dynamic.

Mindfulness, the practice of paying attention to the present moment without judgment, complements gratitude perfectly. In families burdened by intergenerational trauma, the past often intrudes heavily on the present. Anxieties, fears, and unresolved issues can cloud our perception, impacting our relationships and well-being. Mindfulness provides a pathway to escape this cycle, anchoring us in the present moment and freeing us from the grip of past experiences.

Through mindfulness, we learn to observe our thoughts and emotions without judgment, acknowledging them without allowing them to control us.

Mindfulness techniques can be easily integrated into family life. A simple five-minute guided meditation before dinner, even using a children's meditation app, can provide a shared space for calm and reflection. Participating in mindful activities together, such as gardening, cooking, or simply observing nature, can create moments of shared presence and awareness. Mindful breathing exercises can be incorporated into daily routines, providing quick tools for managing stress and anxiety in the moment. These practices not only foster individual well-being but also provide a shared language and approach to managing stress, strengthening the family's resilience in the face of challenges.

The benefits of combining gratitude and mindfulness practices extend far beyond the individual. When family members cultivate these practices, they create a ripple effect, transforming the entire family environment. A family infused with gratitude and mindfulness is better equipped to handle conflict, navigate challenges, and foster stronger, more resilient relationships. It creates a space where vulnerability is welcomed, where emotions are acknowledged and processed constructively, and where healing can begin. This shared practice fosters emotional intelligence within the family, enhancing communication, empathy, and understanding. The ability to approach challenges with a calm, mindful perspective and to appreciate the positive aspects of life, even amidst difficulty, is a powerful tool in breaking free from the cycles of intergenerational trauma.

The integration of gratitude and mindfulness doesn't require a significant time commitment; even short, regular practices can yield substantial benefits. The key is consistency and intentionality. Family members should engage in these practices together, creating a shared experience that reinforces their connection and commitment to well-being.

This shared practice fosters a sense of unity and purpose, further solidifying the family's resilience. This shared engagement is particularly important in families affected by trauma, as it promotes a sense of safety and belonging, essential components of the healing process. Through consistent practice, families can create a supportive environment where emotions are acknowledged, processed, and ultimately released, paving the way for healing and growth.

Furthermore, the practice of gratitude and mindfulness helps to counteract the negative self-talk and critical inner voice that often accompany trauma. These practices encourage a more self-compassionate approach, allowing family members to acknowledge their imperfections and struggles without judgment. This self-compassion then extends to relationships within the family, fostering greater empathy and understanding. By acknowledging and appreciating their own strengths and contributions, family members build self- esteem and resilience, equipping them to face future challenges with greater confidence and grace.

Moreover, incorporating gratitude and mindfulness into family routines can help to establish healthier communication patterns. When individuals are present and mindful, they are better able to listen actively and respond with empathy, rather than reacting defensively or emotionally. This fosters a more open and honest dialogue, creating space for vulnerability and understanding. Through mindful communication, families can address unresolved issues, express needs, and work towards resolution in a constructive and respectful manner.

The long-term effects of incorporating gratitude and mindfulness extend across generations. By modeling these practices, parents pass on invaluable tools for emotional

well-being to their children. These children, in turn, are more likely to develop healthy coping mechanisms, manage stress effectively, and build strong, resilient relationships of their own. In this way, gratitude and mindfulness become a legacy of well-being, breaking the cycle of intergenerational trauma and creating a healthier, happier future for generations to come. This is a significant investment in the family's overall well-being, contributing to a stronger, more connected, and resilient family unit capable of navigating life's challenges with grace and understanding. The cultivation of these practices is not just a therapeutic intervention; it is a transformative family strategy that has the potential to create lasting, positive change.

To further enhance the effectiveness of these practices, consider incorporating journaling into the family routine. Each member can maintain a gratitude journal, recording daily instances of appreciation and positive experiences. This provides a tangible record of progress, reinforcing positive emotions and promoting self-reflection. Similarly, mindfulness journaling can encourage reflection on present moments, emotions, and sensory experiences, deepening the practice and its impact. These journals can become cherished family heirlooms, representing a shared journey of growth and healing, a tangible testament to the transformative power of gratitude and mindfulness.

The path to healing from intergenerational trauma is not a quick fix; it requires ongoing commitment and effort. The incorporation of gratitude and mindfulness is not a standalone solution but rather a crucial component of a comprehensive approach to family well-being. These practices, integrated alongside other strategies for building resilience, communication, and connection, create a powerful synergy that fosters healthier family dynamics and enhances overall well-being for generations to come. The

consistent practice of gratitude and mindfulness provides a foundation of strength, stability, and emotional regulation, empowering families to break free from the burdens of the past and create a brighter future together. This is an investment not just in the present, but in the future well- being of the family, a legacy of love, resilience, and enduring connection.

Passing on Healthy Coping Mechanisms

Passing on healthy coping mechanisms isn't simply about teaching children techniques; it's about modeling them, embedding them into the fabric of family life, and fostering an environment where emotional well-being is prioritized. This is a crucial step in breaking the cycle of intergenerational trauma and building a legacy of resilience. It's about equipping our children with the tools they need not just to survive, but to thrive, even in the face of adversity.

This process begins with self-awareness. Before we can effectively teach our children how to manage stress, anxiety, or difficult emotions, we must first understand and manage our own. Are we modeling healthy coping mechanisms? Or are we unconsciously passing on the very patterns we're hoping to break? If we consistently react to stress with anger, withdrawal, or substance use, our children will likely adopt similar patterns. The first step, therefore, is to honestly assess our own responses to challenging situations. Are we utilizing healthy coping strategies such as exercise, mindfulness, journaling, or seeking support from trusted individuals? If not, this is an area where we need to prioritize personal growth and healing.

Once we've identified our own areas for improvement, we can begin consciously teaching our children healthy coping mechanisms. This isn't a one-time lecture, but an ongoing process integrated into daily life. It begins in infancy, with the consistent provision of comfort and security, teaching them that their feelings are valid and that they have a safe space to express them. As children grow, we can help them develop a vocabulary for their emotions, teaching them to name and identify feelings like sadness, anger, frustration,

and joy. This simple act empowers them to understand and manage their internal experiences.

When children experience challenging emotions, such as anger or frustration, it's crucial to respond with empathy and understanding, rather than criticism or punishment. Instead of dismissing their feelings, we can validate them by saying things like, "I see you're really angry right now. Can you tell me what's making you feel that way?" This validates their feelings and creates a safe space for open communication.

We can then guide them towards healthy ways of expressing their emotions, such as taking deep breaths, going for a walk, or engaging in a calming activity.

The practice of mindfulness can be incredibly beneficial for both children and adults. Mindfulness techniques, such as deep breathing exercises or body scans, can help to calm the nervous system and reduce feelings of overwhelm. Teaching children simple mindfulness practices from a young age can equip them with a valuable tool for managing stress and anxiety throughout their lives. Integrating mindfulness into everyday routines, like taking a few minutes each morning to practice gratitude or focusing on our breath during stressful moments, can cultivate a sense of calm and awareness.

Physical activity is another essential coping mechanism. Exercise releases endorphins, which have mood-boosting effects.

Encourage children to participate in physical activities they enjoy, whether it's playing sports, dancing, or simply running around outside. Make it a family affair, going for walks or bike rides together, creating shared experiences that are both fun and beneficial for emotional well-being.

This creates positive associations with physical activity, establishing it as a go-to method for stress relief.

Creative expression can also serve as a powerful coping mechanism. Encourage children to express themselves through art, music, writing, or any other creative outlet they enjoy. This provides a safe and healthy way to process emotions, reducing feelings of anxiety and promoting self- expression. Even simple activities like drawing or coloring can be helpful for younger children to process their feelings. Creating a dedicated "creative space" in the home can encourage this kind of emotional release and self-expression.

Teaching children problem-solving skills is another crucial aspect of passing on healthy coping mechanisms. When faced with challenges, rather than resorting to emotional outbursts or avoidance, they need to learn how to approach problems calmly and systematically. We can help them develop these skills by asking guiding questions, encouraging them to brainstorm solutions, and helping them to evaluate the potential consequences of different choices. This empowers them to feel in control of their lives and fosters a sense of self-efficacy.

Healthy communication skills are essential for navigating relationships and resolving conflicts. Teaching children how to express their needs assertively, listen actively, and communicate effectively is crucial for their emotional well- being. This includes modeling healthy communication within the family, resolving disagreements calmly and respectfully, and encouraging open and honest communication among family members.

Finally, it's vital to normalize seeking help when needed. This means modeling healthy help-seeking behaviors ourselves, and demonstrating to children that asking for support isn't a sign of weakness, but of strength. It might involve seeking therapy, talking to a trusted friend or family member, or utilizing other available resources. Openly

discussing mental health and emotional well-being destigmatizes these vital aspects of life.

Passing on healthy coping mechanisms is a multifaceted endeavor, requiring a conscious and consistent effort. It's not a one-size-fits-all approach, but rather a tailored process that adapts to the individual needs of each child and the unique dynamics of the family. By focusing on self-awareness, modeling healthy behaviors, and providing children with the tools they need to navigate life's challenges, we can actively contribute to breaking the cycle of intergenerational trauma and create a legacy of resilience and well-being for future generations. This involves ongoing self-reflection, adapting strategies as our children grow, and recognizing that the journey to healing is a continuous process, one that requires patience, empathy, and unwavering commitment. The reward, however, is immeasurable – the gift of emotional well-being, passed down through generations, creating a stronger, healthier, and more resilient family.

This process extends beyond individual coping mechanisms to encompass the broader family system. It means actively fostering open communication within the family, creating a safe space for vulnerability and emotional expression.

Family rituals and traditions can contribute significantly to this sense of security and belonging. Shared activities, such as family dinners, game nights, or weekend outings, strengthen bonds and create positive memories. These create a sense of stability and connection, offering a buffer against life's inevitable challenges.

The importance of seeking professional support cannot be overstated. Therapy, whether individually or as a family, provides a safe and supportive environment to process past trauma and develop healthier coping mechanisms. A therapist can provide guidance and support, equipping both

parents and children with the tools they need to navigate complex emotional challenges. If we recognize unhealthy patterns repeating themselves within our families, professional intervention can be invaluable in breaking these cycles.

Building a legacy of healing is not solely about preventing future trauma, but also about fostering resilience and strength in the face of adversity. It's about teaching children that it's okay to feel a range of emotions, and that they have the inner resources to manage those feelings. It's about emphasizing self-compassion and understanding, helping children to cultivate self-acceptance and self-esteem. It's about creating a family culture where seeking help is normalized and where emotional well-being is prioritized.

In conclusion, passing on healthy coping mechanisms is a long-term investment in the well-being of future generations. It's a journey that requires self-reflection, commitment, and a willingness to actively work towards creating a more emotionally healthy family environment. By actively engaging in this process, we not only empower our children but also contribute to a wider shift toward a more emotionally supportive and resilient society. The legacy we leave behind is not just a collection of possessions, but a legacy of emotional strength and resilience, a legacy of healing that will continue to benefit families for generations to come. This is the true measure of lasting change and the foundation of a truly thriving family.

Chapter 23

Promoting Open Communication Across Generations

Open communication isn't a skill that magically appears; it's cultivated, nurtured, and actively practiced across generations. It requires a conscious effort to break down the walls erected by past hurts and misunderstandings, often stemming from unresolved intergenerational trauma.

Building bridges of understanding necessitates a willingness to listen deeply, to empathize without judgment, and to foster an environment where vulnerability is seen as strength, not weakness. This isn't a passive process; it's about actively creating space for dialogue, even when uncomfortable topics arise. Family meetings, regular check-ins, and intentional time spent together can all contribute to a more connected and communicative family unit. The key is to establish a culture of respect and understanding, one where differing opinions are welcomed as opportunities for growth and learning, not as sources of conflict.

One of the most significant obstacles to open communication across generations is the fear of judgment. Past traumas often lead to a deep-seated fear of vulnerability, making it difficult to share personal experiences and emotions openly. Grandparents may hold onto unresolved pain from their childhood, parents might struggle with the emotional burden of raising children in a challenging world, and children themselves may grapple with the pressures of modern life.

These unaddressed emotions can create significant barriers to communication, resulting in strained relationships and a perpetuation of unhealthy family dynamics. To overcome this, a conscious effort must be made to cultivate an environment of empathy and understanding, where each

individual feels safe enough to express themselves without fear of criticism or rejection.

Active listening plays a crucial role in fostering open communication. It's not simply about hearing the words spoken; it's about understanding the underlying emotions and intentions. It requires fully engaging with the speaker, paying attention to both their verbal and nonverbal cues, and reflecting back what you've heard to ensure understanding.

This process demonstrates respect and validates the speaker's feelings, creating a sense of safety and trust. When individuals feel heard and understood, they are more likely to open up and share their thoughts and feelings freely.

Conversely, when communication is dominated by interruptions, dismissals, or judgments, it creates a climate of fear and distrust, hindering genuine connection.

Furthermore, encouraging empathy is vital in bridging generational gaps. Empathy involves stepping into another person's shoes and understanding their perspective, even if you don't agree with it. It's about acknowledging their feelings and validating their experiences, recognizing that everyone's journey is unique and shaped by their individual circumstances. Empathy fosters compassion and helps to break down preconceived notions and stereotypes that can impede communication. In families where empathy is lacking, misunderstandings and conflicts are more likely to escalate, perpetuating cycles of hurt and resentment.

Cultivating empathy requires active listening, seeking to understand rather than to judge, and practicing patience and tolerance.

Setting clear and healthy boundaries is equally important for promoting open communication. Boundaries define personal limits and expectations, and they are essential for maintaining healthy relationships. Clear boundaries help to

prevent misunderstandings and conflicts by defining acceptable behaviors and interactions. In families where boundaries are unclear or nonexistent, resentment and conflict are more likely to arise. Setting boundaries doesn't mean being uncaring or unsupportive; it means protecting one's emotional and physical well-being while maintaining healthy relationships. It requires open communication about individual needs and expectations, creating a space where everyone feels respected and valued.

Storytelling offers a powerful tool for fostering intergenerational understanding. Sharing personal stories, both positive and negative, can create a sense of connection and empathy. It allows individuals to learn from each other's experiences, fostering a sense of shared history and identity. Stories can provide context for understanding family dynamics and behaviors, highlighting the impact of past trauma on present-day relationships. By sharing their stories, individuals can process their emotions, gain a sense of closure, and promote healing. Creating a safe space for sharing stories, free from judgment and criticism, can be a powerful way to strengthen family bonds and improve communication.

Regular family gatherings, intentionally structured, provide fertile ground for open communication. These gatherings shouldn't be perfunctory events but opportunities for genuine connection. Instead of focusing solely on surface-level interactions, plan activities that encourage deeper engagement. Games that require teamwork, shared storytelling sessions, or collaborative projects can facilitate deeper connections. The structure should prioritize shared experiences, promoting a sense of collective identity and strengthening familial bonds. These gatherings provide a platform to discuss family history, values, and challenges,

fostering a sense of shared understanding and creating opportunities for learning and growth.

Beyond formal gatherings, incorporating daily practices into the fabric of family life can contribute significantly to open communication. Simple acts like sharing meals together, engaging in meaningful conversations, and expressing appreciation for each other can create a culture of connection. These seemingly small gestures build a foundation of trust and mutual respect, setting the stage for more vulnerable and meaningful interactions. A family that values consistent connection, even amidst busy schedules, is a family more equipped to handle conflicts and navigate difficult conversations with grace and understanding.

Addressing past hurts and misunderstandings directly is crucial, but it should always be approached with sensitivity and respect. It is not about assigning blame but about acknowledging the impact of past events on current relationships. Facilitating these conversations might require the guidance of a trained therapist or counselor, especially if deep-seated traumas are involved. The goal is not to rehash old wounds but to acknowledge their impact and work towards healing and reconciliation. This involves a commitment to mutual understanding, forgiveness, and a willingness to move forward.

Technology can be a double-edged sword. While it connects us geographically, it can hinder genuine connection. Over- reliance on digital communication can replace meaningful face-to-face interactions. Therefore, it's vital to maintain a balance, prioritizing quality time spent together over superficial online interactions. Encourage phone calls, video chats, and visits to bridge geographical distances. When using technology, make conscious efforts to engage fully,

avoiding distractions and maintaining eye contact (during video chats) to show engagement and respect.

Finally, remember that building open communication across generations is a continuous journey, not a destination. It requires patience, persistence, and a willingness to adapt and grow. There will be setbacks, disagreements, and challenges along the way, but the commitment to open dialogue and mutual respect will pave the way for healthier, more fulfilling family relationships. The legacy of healing isn't created overnight; it's built through consistent effort and a deep-seated commitment to fostering understanding and empathy across the generations. The rewards—stronger family bonds, improved emotional well-being, and a more resilient future—are well worth the effort. By actively nurturing open communication, we break cycles of trauma, build bridges of understanding, and create a lasting legacy of healing for generations to come. The investment in this process is an investment in the health and well-being of the entire family, extending its positive impact far beyond the immediate present. The strength of a family lies not just in its shared history but in its capacity for ongoing connection, empathy, and understanding.

Breaking Cycles of Dysfunction

The foundation of healing lies in understanding how dysfunctional patterns perpetuate across generations. These patterns, often rooted in unresolved trauma, manifest in various ways, from communication styles and conflict resolution strategies to emotional expression and relationship dynamics. Recognizing these patterns is the crucial first step toward breaking the cycle. It's not about blaming past generations; it's about acknowledging the influence of their experiences on the present, and then consciously choosing a different path.

One common dysfunctional pattern is the avoidance of difficult conversations. Families grappling with unresolved trauma often shy away from addressing sensitive issues, leading to simmering resentment and unspoken hurts. This avoidance can manifest as emotional detachment, indirect communication, or even outright silence. For example, a family might avoid discussing a history of addiction, domestic violence, or significant loss, creating a silent void that impacts subsequent generations. Children growing up in such environments learn to suppress their emotions, avoid conflict, and potentially develop unhealthy coping mechanisms as a result. Breaking this pattern requires a conscious effort to create a space for open and honest communication, even when it's uncomfortable. This involves fostering an environment of trust and empathy where family members feel safe expressing their feelings without fear of judgment or retribution. Facilitating such conversations might require professional guidance, particularly if deep- seated trauma is involved. The process should be gradual and respectful, allowing time for processing and healing.

Another prevalent pattern is the perpetuation of unhealthy relationship dynamics. For instance, a parent who experienced emotional neglect in their childhood might unconsciously replicate that pattern with their own children. This isn't intentional cruelty; it's a manifestation of learned behavior. They might struggle to express affection, provide emotional support, or even set healthy boundaries. Similarly, families with a history of conflict might find themselves perpetually locked in cycles of arguing and tension. This can manifest as constant criticism, belittling remarks, or aggressive behavior, all stemming from unresolved issues and learned coping mechanisms. Breaking these patterns requires self-reflection, identifying the root causes of the unhealthy behaviors, and actively working to develop healthier communication and relationship skills. This often involves seeking professional help, participating in family therapy, and learning new ways to express emotions, manage conflict, and build healthy attachments.

The impact of unhealthy family patterns extends beyond interpersonal relationships. They can also significantly influence an individual's self-esteem and sense of self-worth. For instance, a child raised in a family characterized by criticism and negativity might develop a low self-image and a tendency towards self-doubt. This can lead to difficulties in forming healthy relationships, making sound decisions, and achieving personal goals. Similarly, a family history of trauma can contribute to a heightened sense of anxiety, hypervigilance, or even depression. Breaking these patterns requires fostering a supportive and nurturing environment where individuals feel valued, accepted, and empowered.

This includes offering unconditional love, providing positive reinforcement, and teaching healthy coping mechanisms for managing stress and adversity. Creating a legacy of healing involves actively building a culture of self-compassion and self-acceptance within the family.

Furthermore, understanding the role of intergenerational trauma is vital in breaking these cycles. Unresolved trauma from previous generations often gets passed down, manifesting in subsequent generations as emotional baggage, behavioral patterns, and relationship challenges. This transmission occurs not through direct inheritance of psychological symptoms but through learned behaviors, implicit emotional patterns, and epigenetic modifications.

For instance, a grandparent who survived a war might have difficulty expressing emotions openly. This emotional constriction could then be passed down to their children, who, in turn, might struggle to communicate effectively with their own offspring. The impact extends to physiological effects; studies show that chronic stress and trauma can alter gene expression, increasing vulnerability to mental health conditions in subsequent generations. This understanding highlights the importance of addressing trauma at multiple levels: addressing the individual's current experiences, exploring the family's history, and recognizing the transgenerational nature of trauma's influence.

Breaking these cycles requires a multi-pronged approach. It begins with self-awareness – understanding your own emotional patterns, recognizing triggers, and identifying unhealthy behaviors passed down from previous generations. This self-reflection is crucial, as it lays the foundation for personal healing. Self-compassion plays a vital role here; acknowledging that past experiences have shaped current behaviors without self-criticism is essential for moving forward. This involves identifying the roots of your personal struggles, understanding how they connect to family history, and engaging in practices like mindfulness and self- reflection to gain insight into your emotional patterns.

Journalling, meditation, and therapy can all be effective tools in this process.

Once self-awareness is established, the next step involves establishing healthy boundaries. This means defining personal limits and assertively communicating those limits to others. It's about prioritizing your own well-being without guilt or shame. For instance, setting boundaries might involve limiting contact with family members who engage in toxic behaviors, choosing not to participate in family gatherings that are emotionally draining, or refusing to tolerate verbal abuse or disrespect. Learning to say "no" is a crucial step in protecting your mental and emotional health.

Furthermore, healthy boundaries contribute significantly to the family dynamic. By establishing clear expectations, members can develop a healthier understanding of one another's needs and limits, leading to greater respect and reduced conflict.

Simultaneously, building stronger communication skills is essential. This involves active listening, empathetic responses, and clear and direct communication of thoughts and feelings. This requires practicing effective communication techniques, such as using "I" statements to express personal feelings without blaming others, practicing active listening by seeking clarification and summarizing what has been heard, and using nonverbal cues such as maintaining eye contact and nodding to show engagement. It also entails learning how to manage conflict constructively, which includes avoiding personal attacks, focusing on the issue at hand, and seeking collaborative solutions.

The process of breaking harmful family patterns and fostering healing is not a solitary endeavor. Engaging in family therapy can provide a supportive and structured environment to address these issues collaboratively. Family therapy allows for open dialogue in a safe space, offering the opportunity to work through unresolved conflicts and gain a

deeper understanding of the dynamics within the family. A therapist can guide the family through this process, helping them to identify unhealthy patterns, develop healthier communication skills, and create a more positive and supportive family environment. The therapist's role extends beyond conflict resolution; they provide the crucial framework for emotional expression, self-reflection, and development of healthy coping mechanisms for family members.

Ultimately, creating a legacy of healing is about more than just resolving past hurts. It's about building a future where future generations are empowered to break free from the shackles of past trauma and live more fulfilling lives. This means actively engaging in activities that promote emotional well-being, fostering strong family connections based on mutual respect and understanding, and teaching future generations the importance of self-care, boundary-setting, and open communication. This might involve creating family rituals that promote connection, such as regular family dinners, shared hobbies, or yearly traditions. It also involves modelling healthy emotional regulation and coping strategies for future generations. This long-term perspective emphasizes the importance of creating a culture of emotional health and resilience within the family, ensuring that the positive changes will reverberate across generations. The commitment to healing is not merely a resolution of past hurts, but an ongoing process of creating a legacy of emotional well-being for the future. This journey requires patience, perseverance, and a deep commitment to creating healthier family dynamics for generations to come, a truly meaningful legacy.

Chapter 24

Building Strong Family Bonds

Building strong family bonds requires a conscious and consistent effort, moving beyond mere coexistence to cultivate genuine connection and mutual support. It's about creating a safe haven where vulnerability is embraced, not feared, and where individual needs are respected within the context of the collective well-being. This involves several key strategies, many of which are counter-intuitive to ingrained, often trauma-informed, family patterns.

One crucial element is fostering open and honest communication. This doesn't mean unleashing pent-up emotions in a chaotic outburst; rather, it involves cultivating a culture of respectful dialogue where each family member feels heard and understood. This requires active listening, a skill that goes beyond simply hearing words to truly grasping the underlying emotions and intentions. It involves asking clarifying questions, reflecting back what you've heard to ensure understanding, and validating the other person's feelings, even if you don't necessarily agree with their perspective. For families struggling with past trauma, this might necessitate setting aside dedicated time for communication, perhaps through scheduled family meetings or individual check-ins. Creating a "safe space" – a physical or emotional

environment where family members feel comfortable expressing their thoughts and feelings without fear of judgment or re-
taliation – is paramount. This might involve establishing clear
ground rules for respectful communication, such as avoiding interrupting, name-calling, or personal attacks.

Another critical aspect is the cultivation of empathy and
compassion. Understanding the perspectives of other family
members, even when their actions are hurtful or confusing,
is essential. This requires actively seeking to understand the
root causes of their behavior, considering the impact of past experiences, and acknowledging their inherent worth as individuals. Empathy isn't about condoning harmful behavior, but about
recognizing the human experience behind it. Practicing empathy can involve engaging in perspective-taking exercises, such
as imagining yourself in another family member's shoes and trying to understand their feelings and motivations. It might also
involve actively seeking out information about their experiences
or challenges, showing genuine interest in their lives beyond superficial interactions.

Building strong family bonds also necessitates setting
healthy boundaries. This doesn't imply disengagement or emotional distance, but rather the establishment of clear limits
on acceptable behavior and interactions. Healthy boundaries
protect individual well-being while fostering mutual respect.
Setting boundaries might involve communicating your needs
clearly and assertively, saying "no" to requests that compromise
your values or well-being, and enforcing consequences for
boundary violations. For families with a history of unhealthy
enmeshment or codependency, setting boundaries might be a
particularly challenging but essential step towards healthier relationships. It's important to remember that boundaries are not
about control or manipulation, but about self-respect and mutual consideration.

Furthermore, prioritizing quality time together is crucial. This isn't about filling every moment with structured activities, but rather about creating opportunities for meaningful connection and shared experiences. This could involve engaging in shared hobbies, playing games, going on outings, or simply spending time talking and listening to one

another. Creating family rituals and traditions can further strengthen bonds. These rituals, whether large or small, create a sense of belonging and continuity, providing a framework for shared memories and experiences. They can range from weekly family dinners to annual vacations to simple bedtime stories. These rituals are not merely about adhering to a schedule, but about creating opportunities for connection and shared joy.

Conflict resolution is an inevitable part of family life, and how conflict is managed significantly impacts the strength of family bonds. Instead of avoiding conflict or engaging in destructive arguments, families need to develop healthy conflict resolution strategies. This involves approaching conflict with a spirit of mutual respect, listening actively to understand each other's perspectives, and working collaboratively to find solutions that meet the needs of everyone involved. Compromise, empathy, and a willingness to find common ground are essential elements of effective conflict resolution. Teaching children healthy conflict resolution skills from a young age can prevent negative patterns from developing later in life.

Finally, fostering individual growth and self-care within the family is paramount. Each family member needs to feel supported in their pursuit of their individual goals and passions. This involves respecting individual differences, encouraging self-expression, and providing opportunities for personal growth and development. It also means modeling healthy self-care practices and encouraging family members to prioritize their own emotional and physical well-being.

Recognizing that individual well-being is intrinsically linked to the overall health of the family is critical. A family composed of individuals who are nurtured and supported is far better equipped to navigate challenges and celebrate successes together.

The process of building strong family bonds is an ongoing journey, not a destination. It requires patience, persistence, and a commitment to continuous growth and learning.

Setbacks are inevitable, but the commitment to healing and strengthening relationships will ultimately pay off in the form of deeper connection, increased resilience, and a legacy of love and support for future generations. This process requires self-reflection, empathy, and a willingness to challenge long-held patterns.

Building strong family bonds is not about erasing the past, but about learning from it. It's about consciously choosing to build a different future, a future where the legacy is one of healing, connection, and resilience. This involves accepting imperfections, acknowledging past hurts, and actively working to create a more nurturing and supportive environment. Each family is unique, and the specific strategies needed will vary depending on individual circumstances and challenges. However, the fundamental principles remain consistent: open communication, empathy, healthy boundaries, quality time, effective conflict resolution, and individual growth are all essential components of building a strong and loving family.

Furthermore, seeking professional support can be invaluable in this process. A therapist specializing in family dynamics and trauma can provide guidance, support, and tools to help families navigate challenges, resolve conflicts, and build stronger bonds. Therapy offers a safe and neutral space to explore complex issues, learn healthy communication skills, and develop coping mechanisms for managing difficult emotions. Therapy is not a sign of weakness, but rather a proactive step towards creating a healthier and more fulfilling family life.

The benefits of strong family bonds extend far beyond the immediate family unit. Children who grow up in supportive and loving families are more likely to develop strong self- esteem, healthy relationships, and a greater sense of resilience. They are better equipped to handle life's challenges and to contribute positively to their communities. Building strong family bonds is therefore not merely a personal endeavor, but a contribution to a healthier society. This long-term vision emphasizes the importance of creating a culture of emotional health and resilience within the family, ensuring that the positive changes will reverberate across generations. The commitment to healing is not merely a resolution of past hurts, but an ongoing process of creating a legacy of emotional well-being for the future. This journey requires patience, perseverance, and a deep commitment to creating healthier family dynamics for generations to come, a truly meaningful legacy. It is an investment in the future, a legacy built on love, understanding, and the enduring strength of familial bonds. This investment pays dividends not only for the current generation, but for those who will follow, creating a chain of healing and positive family relationships that continue for years to come. The work is difficult, often requiring confronting painful memories and challenging ingrained behaviors. But the rewards – a family unified by love, mutual respect, and a shared commitment to well-being – are immeasurable. The strength of these bonds will prove invaluable as life's inevitable challenges arise, creating a resilient and supportive network for each family member. The cultivation of this resilience is a gift that continues to provide strength and support for generations to come.

A Vision of Hope

The journey toward healing intergenerational trauma is not a sprint; it's a marathon, a lifelong commitment requiring patience, self-compassion, and unwavering hope. While the process of confronting past hurts and ingrained patterns can be arduous, the potential for transformation and the creation of a brighter future for your family is immense. This is not simply about repairing fractured relationships; it's about building a foundation of emotional well-being that extends beyond your immediate family, impacting generations to come.

Imagine a future where your children and grandchildren experience a childhood free from the shadow of unresolved trauma. Envision a family where open communication flows freely, where emotions are expressed with vulnerability and met with empathy, not judgment. Picture family gatherings filled with laughter, genuine connection, and a shared sense of belonging, a stark contrast to the tension and avoidance that may have characterized past generations. This vision is not unrealistic; it is achievable through consistent effort and a commitment to breaking the cycle of intergenerational pain.

This future requires a paradigm shift in how we approach family dynamics. It requires a conscious decision to prioritize emotional health and well-being over ingrained, often destructive, family patterns. This means actively challenging the belief that emotional pain is something to be endured silently, hidden away, or passed down as an unspoken inheritance. Instead, we must embrace vulnerability as a strength, recognizing that sharing our

experiences, both positive and negative, fosters intimacy and understanding.

The process begins with self-reflection. Understanding your own emotional landscape, identifying the ways in which past traumas have shaped your parenting style, and acknowledging the impact of your family history is paramount. This isn't about blaming past generations; it's about recognizing the powerful influence of inherited patterns and making a conscious choice to interrupt those patterns. This self-awareness is the cornerstone of healing, empowering you to make informed choices about your own behaviors and reactions, breaking free from the cycles that have bound your family for generations.

Once you've begun to understand your own emotional landscape, you can begin to foster healthier communication within your family. This involves active listening, empathy, and a willingness to validate the feelings and experiences of your children. It means creating a safe space where they feel comfortable expressing themselves without fear of judgment or retribution. This safe space is not a passive environment; it requires active participation from each family member, fostering a culture of mutual respect and understanding. This active listening extends beyond simply hearing your child's words; it's about truly understanding their perspective, empathizing with their emotional state, and validating their feelings.

Healthy communication also involves setting clear and consistent boundaries. This is crucial not only for protecting your own emotional well-being but also for teaching your children healthy relationship skills. Setting boundaries isn't about control; it's about protecting your emotional space and ensuring that interactions are respectful and mutually beneficial. It's about teaching your children the importance
of self-respect and asserting their needs in a healthy way, creating a family culture built on mutual respect.

Moreover, consider incorporating healthy coping mechanisms into your family's routine. This might involve engaging in regular family activities that promote connection and relaxation, such as shared meals, outdoor adventures, or creative projects. It could also involve encouraging individual pursuits that foster self-care and emotional regulation, like yoga, meditation, or journaling. These activities cultivate a sense of unity and shared experience, building resilience and strengthening family bonds.

Remember, healing is a journey, not a destination. There will be setbacks and challenges along the way. There will be moments of frustration, anger, and even despair. But it's crucial to persevere, to maintain hope, and to remember that even small steps forward contribute to lasting change.

Celebrate the progress you make, no matter how incremental it may seem. Acknowledge the challenges and setbacks without allowing them to derail your efforts.

This journey requires patience and compassion, not only for yourself but also for your children and other family members. It's a process of collective healing, a journey undertaken together. Recognize that everyone moves at their own pace, and that healing is not a linear process. Be patient with yourself and your family members, allowing each individual the space and time they need to process their emotions and experiences.

Consider seeking professional support as you navigate this journey. A therapist specializing in trauma and intergenerational relationships can provide valuable guidance, tools, and strategies to help you and your family break free from the cycle of pain. Therapy provides a safe

and confidential space to explore complex issues, process difficult emotions, and develop healthier coping mechanisms. It is an investment in your family's future, a commitment to creating a healthier and more fulfilling family dynamic.

Beyond professional support, look for support within your community. Connect with other families who are on a similar journey. Sharing experiences, offering encouragement, and receiving mutual support can be immensely powerful. Find groups, workshops, or online forums where you can connect with others and build a supportive network. The collective strength and shared experiences within a support group can make a profound difference.

The vision of a healed and thriving family is not a pipe dream; it is a tangible goal achievable through consistent effort, self-compassion, and a commitment to breaking the cycle of inter-generational trauma. This is about creating a legacy of emotional well-being, a future where your children and grandchildren can thrive, free from the burdens of the past. It's a commitment to building a family united by love, understanding, and resilience, a family where each member feels safe, seen, and loved uncondi-tionally. This is a legacy worth striving for, a legacy that will res-onate for generations to come, enriching the lives of countless individuals. It is the culmination of a journey, the fulfillment of a long-term vision, the realization of a profound hope. The hope for a future where family bonds are strong, where love thrives, and where healing echoes through generations. It is a vision of hope worth fighting for, a future worth creating. And it starts with you.

Chapter 25

Glossary

This glossary defines key terms used throughout the book:

Attachment: The emotional bond between a child and caregiver, impacting emotional development and future relationships.

Complex Trauma: Trauma resulting from prolonged or repeated exposure to overwhelming adversity.

Emotional Regulation: The ability to manage and respond to one's emotions in a healthy way.

Epigenetics: The study of how environmental factors influence gene expression without altering DNA sequence. **Intergenerational Trauma:** The transmission of trauma and its effects across generations.

Mindfulness: Paying attention to the present moment without judgment.

Non-Violent Communication (NVC): A communication method that emphasizes empathy and understanding.

Resilience: The ability to recover from adversity and bounce back from challenging situations.

Trauma: A deeply distressing or disturbing experience.

Trauma-Informed Care: An approach to care that recognizes and responds to the impact of trauma on individuals.

References

[Include a complete list of references cited in the book, following a consistent citation style (e.g., APA, MLA).] This section will include academic journal articles, books, and any other credible sources referenced within the text.

Author Biography

[Author Name] is a Licensed Therapist and Family Counselor specializing in trauma and intergenerational relationships. With [Number] years of experience, [He/She/They] have dedicated their career to helping families heal from the lasting effects of trauma. [He/She/They] have a particular interest in [Mention specific areas of expertise or interest within trauma therapy, e.g., attachment theory, family systems therapy]. Beyond clinical practice, [Author Name] is a passionate advocate for [Mention advocacy work or related activities] and has previously authored [Mention previous publications, if any]. [He/She/They] are committed to empowering individuals and families to build healthier, more resilient relationships and break free from the cycles of generational trauma. [Optional: Add contact information or website, if appropriate].